They Called Me Mr. Scales

Phil Scales

LEEMON Publishing—Madison, WI
ISBN: 979-8-218-24997-7
Library of Congress Control Number: 2023916811
Title: *They Called Me Mr. Scales*
Author: Phil Scales
Digital distribution | 2023
Paperback | 2023

Published in the United States by New Book Authors

Dedication

Table of Contents

Prologue

Martin Luther King Jr. once said, "Judge a man by the content of his character and not by the color of his skin."

I have always kept these important words firmly rooted in the front of my mind as I made my journey through life. However, it seems that our young people today are doing just the opposite. They want to reside inside safe places where no one would say anything hurtful to them or about them. Our young always seem strong and outspoken in a group of their peers, but what happens to the individual Black person who moves out of that comfort zone and ends up being the only Black person on the job? Most people believe that they sell out and become the Oreo in the room (black on the outside and white on the inside); sometimes that happens, but most of the time, it does not. These resilient strong individuals with unwavering spirits stand their ground through racism and hatefulness. Most of these strong people become role models to young kids who may have never had a Black student or a Black teacher in their class. The only thing they may know about Black people is what they see on TV or the news; most of the time, it's unpleasant and biased. Throughout the years, the portrayal of Black people by prejudiced sources has created a picture where blacks are represented as violent offenders, whereas the actual perpetrators are shown as victims. Nevertheless, the reality is quite contradictory and often bitter. I am one of those people who dared to walk out of my comfort zone into a world that was not entirely accepting of Black America, and I went alone and unafraid. This is my story.

Chapter One
They called me Mr. Scales

MY story begins in 1961 when I was in 4th grade and had just moved to Pittsburgh from West Homestead. I lived in a community in Pittsburgh called Glenwood. There were three small communities, Glenwood, Glen-Hazel, and Hazelwood, which were surrounded by three steel mills - US Steel, Jones & Lockman, and Mesta Mills. The B&O railroad ran straight through Glenwood, and the racial dynamics of the community were fifty percent Black and fifty percent white. The reason I'm starting with the fourth grade is because it was a defining part of my life when I experienced unabashed bullying for the first time.

I missed just one day of school between kindergarten and 4th grade, and that was the day that they handed out musical instruments to the students. When I went to school the next day, I asked the teacher if I could play the trumpet; but all of them were taken, so I asked to play the sax, but everything was out except the violin. I did not want to play violin because only the girls were playing this instrument, and my neighborhood was unforgiving of foolishness, and this would be foolish.

Mr. Kirkman told me that I could play the violin for a year, and then I could switch to a different instrument, so I agreed to the plan. We got the instruments for free, but we would be responsible for any damages.

The school even paid for the new strings. My Dad told my brothers and me that he never wanted to see us fighting or horse playing around with the instruments because he could not afford to pay for the repairs. I had lessons on Tuesday and Thursday, and every Tuesday and Thursday after school, I would run home with the violin tucked under my arm because the kids were throwing rocks at me and my violin. This went on for about three weeks until I had enough and remembered that Dad said that he did not want to see me fighting with the violin. So, one day after my Tuesday lesson, I came out of school and the kids were, as usual, calling me sissy Scales and throwing rocks at me again.

I ran home as fast as I could and put the violin on the kitchen table so that when Dad got home, he would see the violin on the table. Then I ran back to school, looked at the biggest kid, and said, now, what did you say? The big kid beat me to the ground, but I kept getting up and would not quit, so the kid just walked away. I was never bullied again. I had only been in Pittsburgh for about six months, and I didn't have many friends, but it's funny because the guys I fought with became my best friends. The next week a kid stopped playing the trumpet, and Mr. Kirkman called me in to switch instruments, but I had fallen in love with the violin. So, I decided to continue playing the violin and made up my mind to work hard to become the best violinist in the tri-community.

My First Taste of Racism

I was in seventh grade and was on my way to becoming a good violinist, but I was way ahead of all my classmates in the orchestra, so Mr. Kirkman started me on viola as well. I was also good at sports, mainly baseball, football, and swimming. Football was king in the tri-community because everyone went to the same high school, and we were all about sports.

My first love was an Italian girl named Linda, who also was a great friend. She was somewhat of a tomboy, but we would laugh, talk, and just hang out. One day when we were at the swimming pool, her parents came by and took her home. I was unbothered by the situation and didn't think anything about it because it had happened before, but about half an hour later, my brother came up to me and said that I needed to be home. I walked in the door and mom said your father wants to talk to you upstairs.

This was way scary because back in the sixties, dads did not do a lot of talking to the kids; it was always on Mom. So, I went into the bedroom, and my dad said that Linda's parents had just left, and that her mother said that she did not want her daughter dating a colored boy (this is what we called ourselves in the sixties), and if we did not stop then she would be forced to send her daughter to Cleveland. I was in shock, and I became afraid, not just because of what Linda's Mom said, but what was my dad going to say? My Dad said, "Phil, in this house, your mom and all your siblings will respect anyone that you bring into this house, but you and your friend have a problem to solve."

After that incident, we decided to just be friends, which meant that it was over. Still, all through high school, I never stopped loving her through furtive glances. It would be a long time before I put myself in that position again.

My Dream

I knew in 8th grade that I wanted to be a music teacher and an orchestra conductor. My love for conducting and classical music came at a young age. I was probably just four years old when I developed a deep love for watching two things, the Lawrence Welk Show, and cartoons. I was fascinated by the way Lawrence Welk controlled the orchestra with a long white baton and seemed to enjoy every moment. Classical music was instilled in me by way of Saturday morning cartoons. Most of the shows played classical music, but I didn't know the names of most of the pieces until I started playing the violin, which opened a new world for me. When I first saw Fantasia, I thought I had died and gone to heaven. Then I heard the music of the Lone Ranger, and I couldn't wait to direct the William Tell Overture someday.

I went to the orchestra teacher and asked what steps would help me achieve my goal. He smiled and told me that learning and playing most instruments would be helpful. So, I started learning the cello and invested putting more time into playing the violin and viola. A year later, I was concertmaster of the high school orchestra, and I played viola in the all-city orchestra in Pittsburgh. I also auditioned and was selected for the school for musical talent in Pittsburgh.

This school was on Saturdays and ran from 8-12. We had four classes, theory, ensemble, private lesson, and a discovery class where each ensemble class would perform for the rest of the school. My private teacher at the school was the principal violist of the Pittsburgh Symphony. So, as you can see, my life was going smoothly. I played violin, viola, cello, and baritone horn, and was on the football and baseball team. I was also dating Rachel, but then the bottom fell out.

April 4, 1968

The day started with a lot of excitement because my birthday was on April 7, which fell on a Sunday, so Rachel decided to throw a birthday party with just a few close friends on Thursday night at 7:00 pm to celebrate my 16th birthday. Rachel was the only biracial girl in the school, and she was a year behind me. She played clarinet in the band and was very shy and quiet. We made a good-looking couple, and I persuaded her into trying out for the cheerleading squad. She made the team, and one of her captains was Linda. At about 6:15 on April 4, 1968, it came across the TV that Martin Luther King Jr. had been assassinated. I walked the two miles to Rachel's house, and it seemed like everyone was starting to get very unsettled and started pouring into the street. There was chaos everywhere. I got to Rachel's house around 7:00, and by that time, the fires had begun. The main street, 2nd Avenue, ran from Hazelwood to downtown Pittsburgh (three miles) and was on fire. It seemed like every other business was on fire, and other parts of the city were burning too.

The Mayor of Pittsburgh put a curfew on the city starting at 8:00 pm. I panicked, so I called my dad to come and pick me up because I did not want to walk the streets alone. As far as I can remember this was the first time that I had ever been afraid in my neighborhood. Dad got there in about 20 minutes, and we took the back roads home. There was smoke everywhere, and stores were still burning, and I felt terrible because the store owners (white and black) had done nothing to deserve this. I thought about how the white community would respond. As we passed the grade school, three shots went flying over the car, Dad slammed on the brakes and jumped out of the car, and I heard three quick shots; Dad was shooting back. He got back in the car, and we never said a word.

Lines are Drawn

The next day as I walked to the school, I saw all the destruction from the fires. The storefronts of Hazelwood were burned to the ground (and they were never rebuilt). The school grounds were a lot different this morning; usually, you would have groups of students, black and white talking together, but not this morning. The bell rang and the students went inside, but most of the white students did not go inside. They stayed across the street and yelled at us to come out and get it on. I could understand their frustration because their parents' livelihood had been burnt down for something that they hadn't taken part in.

So, we did come out, and I do not know why I went out, but everything was just out of control. Before anyone knew what had happened, someone threw a brick into the crowd, and a brawl ensued. After about twenty minutes, the police vans rolled up and the police had 3-foot riot sticks, and they meant business. Our school Gladstone High was never the same for the next two years, and the school split right down the middle on race.

Most of the white students left the high school and the ones that stayed stopped playing any sports or being involved in any activities. Our sports teams went from 50/50% to 98/2% Black to white. In my senior year, we had a total of 23 players (22 black and one white) on the football team. (I'm number 15, and my brother Aaron (nicknamed Buster or Bus) is 14).

1969 Football Team

We played in the city league with powerhouse teams like Westinghouse, Peabody, Carrick, and Taylor Allderdice. All these schools had over 2,500 students, and now Gladstone was under 500 students. We had five seniors on the football team, and I played every down of every game, offense, and defense. I never left the field during the game.

As I mentioned before, football was king in the neighborhood, and Gladstone had never had a losing season. Well, after our first four games, we were 0-4 and we were the talk of the community. I played tailback, and Buster played the slot. One night in bed (we shared a bed for 18 years), Bus said that we could not lose another game and I agreed. Then he said: then run faster, and I said, then catch the damn ball. The next game (homecoming), Bus ran for four touchdowns, and I had three, and we beat Langley High 49-0. We won our last four games and ended up 4-4, not a losing season. I was chosen by the coaches as the MVP, and I went to a dinner for all the MVPs in the city. It was a great honor to represent this team because we were true underdogs in every game, and we never stopped fighting.

One Brave Teacher

In my senior year, I had a Civics class, and the teacher was Dr. Ted Soens. He was the hardest teacher in the school but was the most respected by the students. If you got a C from him, you were happy because he made you work to your potential and did not pander to slackers. The first week of my senior year, September 1969, Dr. Soens walked into the Civics class and put two 35mm cameras on the front table. He said, your semester assignment is to make a documentary film of the riots and turmoil that hit our school and community. He further added that we would work together (28 in class, 14 black, 14 white) and go out into the community to record the feelings of the community members.

He then left the classroom. We sat there until the bell rang, and then we went to our next class. The next day in class, Dr. Soens didn't appear, but the cameras were still on the table. The bell rang and we went to our next class. On the third day I began to think, hey, I need this class to go to college, and so does Bus, so the class began talking to each other about how this might be fun. So, we started working together, and everyone in the school noticed that this group had put differences aside so that they could work together.

This project reunited our class, and we made the film. Dr. Soens held an Oscar Awards Night, where our film was screened for the student body and parents. It was a great night, and the class of '70 finally began to heal. During the making of the film, the class of '70 reemerged as the leaders of the school again, and we elected our class officers (three white and two black). My brother Buster was elected Vice President, which made me so proud of him.

Our senior class got had gotten so close that when we had our senior skip day, ¾ of the school skipped with us. The next day no one got in trouble because that was the first time the school had done anything together in two years.

I ended my baseball career at Gladstone, and I was 7-2 as a pitcher. I secured a baseball scholarship for college as I was a good hitter and leadoff batter. We were down to our last week at Gladstone High School, and my college plans were in place. I was going to Sterling College in Kansas.

Three days before graduation, the principal asked me if I would play a violin solo on commencement night, and I said that I would be happy to play. On graduation night, we were all lined up in the back, and some of us were getting our yearbooks signed. Linda signed my yearbook, and this is what she wrote. "To Phil-The greatest and most handsome dude I ever knew in all my years at Gladstone. Don't ever forget me. Remember the wonderful and bad times me and you had, it was fun while it lasted. So, you be good and to Rachel too! I hope you and she make it through. Good Luck. Love Always '70 Linda." We embraced each other, knowing that this may be the last time we would ever see each other again (and it was). My violin solo was right before we were handed out the diplomas, and this would be the last time that I played for my classmates.

The Scales Brothers

I started playing and three bars into the piece, my E string broke. The principal asked what we should do now, and I said that I would go backstage and change the string. I said that he could start handing out the diplomas until I got it fixed, so that is what we did. I came back out on stage to finish my solo, but eight bars into the piece, the string broke again. I walked off stage, and the principal started handing out the diplomas again.

I was infuriated by the situation, and I felt like smashing my violin, but I heard a voice behind me; it was Mom. She asked me if I was all right, and I replied yes.

She then asked, "Are you going to get through this?"

And I again said yes. I stood off stage, and the principal saw me and stopped handing out the diplomas again. This time I nailed the piece and got a standing ovation from my classmates, but to this day, I don't know if I got the ovation because it was good or if they were glad that I was finished, because it took 45 minutes to get it done.

What this class did for the school and community was reflected in the message that our principal Francis Haggerty wrote in our yearbook. "Congratulations to the class of 1970. Your class has been a shining example of what can be accomplished through togetherness. Togetherness is the cohesive force of unity, and your class has so admirably demonstrated a unity that was beneficial to all. This spirit of togetherness, when put into practice, accomplishes the unbelievable. It is the moving force of great nations. It is the bond that keeps our nation safe from aggression. Through togetherness, the quiet voice of the people becomes a roar. It is the unmeasured intangible that motivates the underdog to athletic upsets. The help and effort expended by you have helped make your class of 1970 one of Gladstone's finest. You should feel a deep sense of pride and accomplishment. Once again, congratulations and success in the future."

Off to College

It was August 15, 1970, and my dad was dropping me off at the airport to fly to Kansas to start my college career. I had been accepted to eight different colleges, and I chose to go to Sterling College because they wrote to me every day, and it would be a break from competing with my brother for four more years. As we arrived at the airport, I got my things out of the car, and Dad said, "Remember who you are and where you come from."

I said I would, and I hugged my dad (for the first time, and it startled him). I told him that I loved him, and he said that he was proud of me.

I had never been on an airplane before, and I had a three-hour layover in Chicago, so I did a little people-watching. I made eye contact with this young lady and smiled, then we both got on the plane together because we were flying on standby. When I arrived in

Wichita, KS, I was to call the college, and someone would come and pick me up. The college was 100 miles away and it was already dark. I noticed that the girl from Chicago was also waiting for someone, so I went to her and introduced myself, and she did the same. She had an accent that sounded like it was from the islands, so I asked her where she was from, and she said Kingston, Jamaica. The lady with the Jamaican accent was going to Sterling College and her name was Carell Gordon. I did not know at this time that she and I would be connected for the rest of our lives.

Chapter Two
Sterling College

The drive from the airport was very boring because it was late at night, and I could not see anything. I got to the dorm, got my door key, and hit the bed. Three other guys were sleeping, so I just slept in my clothes that night. We were all up early the next morning, and we looked out the windows, and all we could see were cornfields. My roommates were from Florida, one from Cocoa Beach (Stan-6'3"-220 football player), and the other two were from Fort Lauderdale. (Ike-5'10"-180-football; Slim-track).

The guys from Florida had never seen snow before and were in for a shock. Sterling had 6 black men and 5 black women on campus before our class arrived. Sterling College's athletic department wanted to be competitive in the KCAC conference, so they recruited 45 black men (all athletes) to help achieve this goal.

They also brought one Black lady who was not an athlete (Carell). I do not think the professors at Sterling even knew that they would have that many minorities on campus because they were not prepared. We started football practice the next day. I was there on a football, baseball, and music scholarship, so I was mentally ready for this and ready to go.

The athletes were much bigger in college. I stood 5'6" and weighed 175 pounds but ran a 4.6 forty-yard dash. The head coach called me in and asked about my goals. I told him that I wanted to work hard to be a starter in football and baseball. He looked at me and said, "Well, that's great, but I just had two walk-ons (two guys over 6 feet and over 200 pounds), and we need another scholarship, so would you be willing to give yours up?"

I said no, and the coach then said that my equipment was in my locker. I went to my locker and put my pads on, but my helmet was missing a face mask. I went to the equipment manager and asked for one. He said that they had over 80 players on the field and that they had run out, but he would order some.

I ran out onto the field and saw that I was the only one without a face mask. We worked on hand shield contact, and the seniors were doing all the screaming and hitting. Every time I would do a drill, I would get blasted in the face as I had no face mask. This went on for two days, and we practiced three times a day. My face was bruised, and my lips were split. I think they bloodied my nose three or more times. They wanted me to quit and give up my scholarship, but I was from Glenwood, and we did not quit.

In the last drill of the day, a senior (free safety Blair) pounded me in the face, and I slammed him to the ground and would not let him up. The coaches came over and broke it up. The next day at practice, I had a face mask. Sterling was a huge cultural difference for the Black athletes from the south, and most went back home. Sterling frowned on two things: smoking and interracial dating. The ladies had a key system, where freshmen, sophomores, and juniors had to be in at 9:00 on the weekday and 11:00 on the weekend. The senior women had to be in at 11 on the weekdays and midnight on the weekends.

The men did not have a key system, but what do you do when all the ladies are in the dorm? Well, you go downtown to the local bar and play pool. It was an exciting pastime, but with so many Black people, it made the local people nervous, and sometimes fights would break out. When that would happen, the Dean of Men (Bill Calderwood) would always come to the dorm and wake up all the Black men to see if he could find out who was fighting downtown. I always voiced my opinion on this because I thought it was somewhat racist to wake up every black man, and that would drive him up a wall. But the Dean of Men did not like Phil Scales. Little did I know that this man and I would knock heads for the next four years.

My Major

I wanted my Major to be music, but I found out that it would take five years to graduate with a music degree. So, I met with my music advisor, Professor Gordon, and told him that I wanted to do it in four. I was the first athlete and music person to try to graduate in just four years. Professor Gordon looked at me and said, "Do you think you can do that."

And I replied, "That's the plan."

So, for the next three hours, we mapped out every class that I would have to take to stay on course to graduate in '74. It came out to 17-19 hours every semester for the next four years.

I was the only Black student in the music department. In my first spring semester, the whole music department went on tour for 10 days, and we stayed in people's homes. I asked Prof. Gordon if he ever told the people that I was Black, and he said no, but the people would come up to me and say, you must be Phil Scales. I quickly started to realize why no one majored in music and was active in sports simultaneously because both interests definitely clashed. I had marching band the first semester, and to get an A out of the class, you had to march at half-time of the football games. I tried to explain to Prof. Gordon that I could not leave the team to march in the half-time show. He said that he had never had that problem before and that I had to work it out. Well, I had marching band for four semesters, and the highest grade I ever got was a B because I was on the football team.

We had to be on the field at 3:45 for football (no excuses) every day, but on Tuesdays, I had piano lessons from 3:00-4:00, so I ran extra laps after practice every Tuesday. I could have whined and cried about it, but that was the rule, so I dealt with it. The other conflict that I had with sports and music would pop up in the spring during baseball season. I loved playing baseball, and the first time that I met Coach Gleason, he asked what position I wanted to play, and I told him that I was a pitcher, and he replied that he had never had a colored pitcher before. There was a senior, Kent Davidson, who played centerfield and was the leadoff batter, and the coach moved Kent to short-stop and put me in his spot, so I played centerfield and was the second batter up after Kent. We were the best first and second batters in the league. Kent also played basketball and won senior athlete of the year. After he won that award, I knew that was now my goal for my senior year.

I was the only Black player on the team for two years. In the spring we would have our piano recitals, and a lot of times, it would fall on the day of our baseball games. The games were doubleheaders with a 30-minute break in between the games, so I would schedule my recital piece in between the games. Everyone would be dressed up, and I would come in with my baseball uniform on. Most of the time, my uniform would be covered with dirt, but I would sit at the piano bench and play my solo, then I would hustle back to the ball field for the second game. In my freshmen year on the baseball team, I hit in the winning run to help Sterling win its first KCAC Championship ever. I then went to my recital and was so excited that I almost forgot what I was going to play. (This team was later inducted into the Sterling College Sports Hall of Fame in 2010.)

Life on Campus

My first year in football was a big adjustment because we had over 80 players, and to get any playing time as a freshman would be hard. So,

I decided to learn all the offensive back plays and all the secondary positions because I felt that this would be my best chance of playing. My goal was to practice hard enough that I could make the special teams, which I did, but I was also back up to the offensive running back and backup secondary man. My roommate, Ike Brown, was a starter on the left cornerback spot, and five minutes before our second game, he sprained his ankle. Coach came to me and said, "Scales, you're in."

I ran out on the field, and I got right up in the wide receivers' faces. When the ball was snapped, I saw the quarterback pitch the ball out to the running back, and I made a mad dash to tackle him, but he pulled up and threw a 60-yard pass to my man. (Touchdown!). I ran over to the sidelines, and Coach Bennett said, "Welcome to college football."

I stood on the sidelines, hoping that I would get another chance, but it did not seem likely. When it was the defense's turn to go back out, I hesitated, and the coach said, "Get your ass back out there."

The first thing I did when the ball was snapped was forearm my receiver right in the mouth. That was my way of saying "nice catch." We won the game, and my man did not catch another pass. In our fifth game of my freshman year, we were pretty banged up, on both sides of the ball, and I ended up playing slot-back and right corner. I caught two passes and played a solid game on defense.

After the game, Coach told me that I had done a great job of playing both positions, but next year he would like me to decide on playing on the O side of the ball or the D side of the ball. I always did like to hit people, so I played defense for the next three years. In the second season of football, I played special teams and backup for anyone in the secondary that was hurt or benched. We were having a good season at 4-2, and we were playing Friends University from Wichita. They were at the top of the division and beating us 22-3 at the half because they had a good running game, and their 6'4" tight end was killing us. Our rover could not stay with him, and he killed us in the first half. Friends' game plan was not to have to throw the ball to their wideouts, because we had two of the best corners in the conference. (Ike Brown & Bill Portes, who was later drafted by the Browns). At the half, the defensive back coach was shouting at the top of his voice, "Who can watch the tight end because he is killing us?"

I stood up and said, "I got him."

But the coach kept shouting, and I said again, "I got him."

Coach looked down at me (he was 6'5") and said, "All right, you're in."

Ike hit me on the head and said, "Shut him down."

I went at him on play one, and he was not as fast as me, so I played him straight up the rest of the game. We had them pinned back on their three-yard line, and my tight end blocked down, and I ran off his butt to the quarterback and got him for a safety. We then shut down their running game, and I had the tight end covered, so they had to throw at their wideout, and that played right into our hands. They threw the ball 22 times in the second half, but only connected on 7 for 40 yards. Ike had two picks and Bill had one. We shut them completely down, and on the last play of the game they were behind 25-22, and they threw a Hail Mary, and Ike intercepted the ball going out of bounds.

The receiver pushed Ike so hard in the back that he fell and rolled on the cinder track field. I was right there, so I tackled the receiver, and both benches cleared, and we fought for ten minutes. After the coaches broke everything up, we went to our locker room, where Ike was sitting in front of his locker with most of his pads off. He looked up and said, "Did I miss a meeting?"

When the guy knocked Ike down, he jumped up and ran to the locker room and did not know that we were fighting for him.

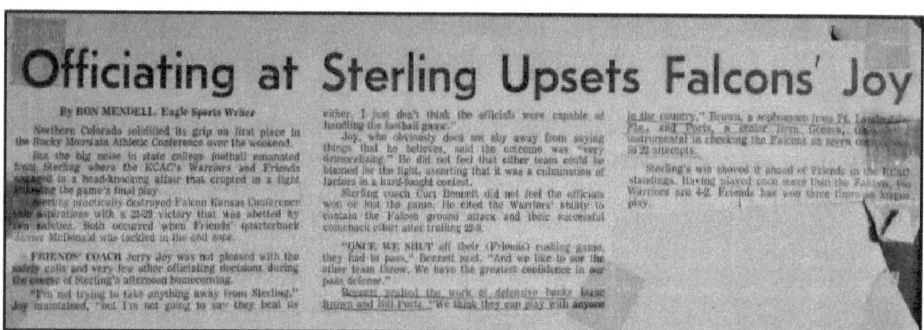

Officiating at Sterling Upsets Falcons' Joy

By RON MENDELL, Eagle Sports Writer

Northern Colorado solidified its grip on first place in the Rocky Mountain Athletic Conference over the weekend.

But the big noise in state college football emanated from Sterling where the KCAC's Warriors and Friends engaged in a head-knocking affair that erupted in a fight following the game's final play.

Sterling practically destroyed Falcon Kansas Conference title aspirations with a 25-22 victory that was abetted by two safeties. Both occurred when Friends' quarterback James McDonald was tackled in the end zone.

FRIENDS' COACH Jerry Joy was not pleased with the safety calls and very few other officiating decisions during the course of Sterling's afternoon homecoming.

"I'm not trying to take anything away from Sterling," Joy maintained, "but I'm not going to say they beat us either. I just don't think the officials were capable of handling the football game."

Joy, who obviously does not shy away from saying things that he believes, said the outcome was "very demoralizing." He did not feel that either team could be blamed for the fight, asserting that it was a culmination of factors in a hard-fought contest.

Sterling coach Curt Bennett did not feel the officials won or lost the game. He cited the Warriors' ability to contain the Falcon ground attack and their successful comeback effort after trailing 22-0.

"ONCE WE SHUT off their (Friends) rushing game, they had to pass," Bennett said. "And we like to see the other team throw. We have the greatest confidence in our pass defense."

Bennett praised the work of defensive backs Isaac Brown and Bill Portz. "We think they can play with anyone in the country." Brown, a sophomore from Ft. Lauderdale, Fla., and Portz, a senior from Geneva, were instrumental in checking the Falcons on seven of 22 attempts.

Sterling's win shoved it ahead of Friends in the KCAC standings. Having played once more than the Falcons, the Warriors are 4-2. Friends has won three times in league play.

That was the start of the biggest rivalry in the KCAC, Friends vs. Sterling, and it still exists today. I ended the season at the Rover spot. I loved playing the Rover position because it put me right in the middle of the action. I had lettered for the second year, but I was not a starter and did not know if I would be one until the roster for the next season came out.

KCAC - should have an outstanding year.
EARL DONALSON - 6'0", 178 lb. Jr. - Titusville, Fla. Started last year. . .with a full year of experience Earl should be an excellent target for the SC Quarterbacks.
DAVE FATH - 5'9", 192 lb. Sr. - Jeannette, Pa. Voted outstanding offensive lineman by teammates in 1972. . . great blocker. . .great attitude.
TIM ADAIR - 5'11", 175 lb. Sr. - Kingsdown, Ks. Pound for pound our most dedicated athlete. . .3 year starter. . . will have a great year.
MIKE ANDERSON - 5'10", 165 lb. Sr. - Haxton, Colo. Mike plays the tightback position for the Warriors. . . must be most versitile athlete. . .2nd leading pass receiver. . .great attitude.
ERNIE SPORE - 5'11", 215 lb. Sr. - Sterling, Ks. Ernie returns as a three year starter. . .has great power. . .great blocker.
BILL HEADLEE - 6'1", 210 lb. Soph. - Kodaka, S.D. Bill has the size to become a devastating fullback. . .an outstanding student with a great future as a Warrior.
TED STEWART - 5'10", 190 lb. Soph. - Haven, Ks. Started as a freshman at tailback. . .has great power and balance. . .will be a great one for SC.
MIKE McCLURE - 5'8", 170 lb. Sr. - Dewey, Okla. AFter transferring from Cowley County Juco, Mike will be vying for the starting QB position this fall. . .a 63% passer makes him a top candidate.
WAYNE COTTMAN - 6'0", 180 lb. Sr. - Warminster, Pa. Wayne was the 2nd leading punter in the KCAC in 1971 . . .will share the QB duties with McClure in 1972.

OTHER POTENTIAL OFFENSIVE STARTERS

LEN CORYEA - 6'2", 190 lb. Jr. - Greenville, Pa.
TIM KOEHN - 6'2", 215 lb. Soph. - Lakewood, Colo.
JIM KRALIK - 6'0", 185 lb. Sr. - Latrobe, Pa.
ROGER COLDREN - 6'0", 210 lb. Jr. - Export, Pa.

RETURNING DEFENSE

IKE BROWN - 5'11", 170 lb. Jr. - Ft. Lauderdale, Fla. Two year starter for the Warriors. . .has great speed and quickness. . .should have an outstanding year as corner back.
PHIL SCALES - 5'6", 176 lb. Jr. - Pittsburg, Pa. Most versatile player in 1971. . .plays all defensive backfield positions well. . .will play rover this fall.
MARK McCRORY - 6'0", 190 lb. Sr. - Denison, Ks. 3 year letterman, Mark will be vying for the starting LB position this fall. . .won Olsen Award for outstanding scholastic athlete.
JEFF SPARAGANA - 5'10½", 210 lb. Soph. - Reading, Pa. Moved into starting line up last fall. . .great hitter. . . should have a great year in 1972.
GALEN CRABBS - 6'0", 195 lb. Soph. - Hutchinson, Ks. Will be going after punting duties. . .also counted on strongly as starting linebacker. . .great hitter.
HOWARD JACKSON - 6'2", 210 lb. Jr. - Brownstown,

The roster came out and read: "Phil Scales-5'6", 176 lbs. Pittsburgh Pa. The most versatile player in 1971, plays all defensive backfield positions well and will play Rover this year." When my junior year started, we felt like we were one player away from being a good defensive football team. The position we needed was a right cornerback, and we had a Black player come to Sterling from Pittsburgh. This guy played for Westinghouse when I was a senior (he was a sophomore) at Gladstone, his name was Garry Sims, and we became very tight. Gary had raw talent, and Ike and I consistently stayed in Gary's ear to smooth that raw talent out. The defense found that missing piece.

Defensive Captain

We ended my junior season at 7-2, which was the best record that Sterling had ever recorded. My best game was against Tabor University, where they had senior black twins who were great athletes. The best of the two was Roland Lawrence (who was later drafted by the Atlanta Falcons), who ran the 100-yard dash in 9.9 seconds. They called him Bay Lawrence because it seemed like he was as fast as a horse. Bay would start pulling away from you, and when he hit the ten-yard line, he would turn and go in backward on you and then drop the ball by your foot when he crossed the goal line. Our game plan was to take Bay out of the game, and that was my job. Usually, 45 minutes before game time, all the Black athletes on both sides would get together, because there were so few of us that we knew each other, and it was a great fellowship time.

I did not go out, because I was totally in a zone for this game. I had in my mind all week that Bay would not run in backward on me. I did not want to talk to him, and I didn't want to see him before the game. We beat Tabor 21-7, and Bay did not catch a pass on me (0-10). Every time a pass came his way, I was able to block it. Bay tried to talk to me the whole game, but I never responded. The last pass that I guarded Bay on was a quick out, and he had me beat, so I dove in the air and just got the ball on my fingertips to block it away. With 2 minutes left in the game, Coach Bennett took me out in appreciation for the game that I played, and Ike had the duty of covering Bay for the remaining

2 minutes. Bay caught one on Ike, and I never brought it up. Bay came up to me after the game and said, "I tried to get you, Scales."

And we embraced and walked away. My senior year was very satisfying; we ended up with a record of 6-3, but it should have been 8-1 or 9-0. The defense was ranked 21st in the country, and the secondary (Ike, Gary, Zizzler, and I) was ranked 7th in the country.

Defensively, the conference is Sterling's! In the areas of total defense, rushing defense, and passing defense the Warriors are ranked number one. Not only that, but in the official NAIA statistics for six games, The Warriors are ranked in total defense and passing defense nationally. In total defense, Sterling is ranked seventh in Division II and is ranked twenty-first among all NAIA schools. In passing defense, Sterling is ranked third in Division II and seventh overall among NAIA schools. Achievements like these just leave you speechless. Anyway, Congratulations, Warrior defense.

The class of '74 football team had three black football players from the 45 players that started four years earlier.

The tallest Black athlete (Stan Collins) and the Black athlete behind me (Ike Brown) were my roommates.

Classes

My campus life was hard sometimes, but I chose to go to Sterling because of the small teacher-to-student ratio. We did not have tutors or professors who let you skip class because you were a good athlete. We were there on our merit, and that is why a lot of guys left. Some of the professors went out of their way to help Black students, but I did not get this help from the music department.

One of the teachers who really cared about us was our English professor, Ms. Binki, with whom we had classes on Mondays, Wednesdays, and Fridays at 7:45 in the morning. She would call over to the dorm to get us up so we wouldn't miss her class, but the music department did nothing to make things better for me. I worked hard in the department and played several different instruments during my time there. I played French horn in the concert band, baritone horn and trumpet in the pep band, oboe in ensemble groups, and Bari-sax in a jazz band. A famous bandleader, Clark Terry, came to Sterling, and I played Bari-sax with his group. I also directed the pep band at the basketball games, so you can see I was committed and involved. I had thirty music classes at Sterling and only received three A's out of all the classes, but when I earned my master's degree later, I had 42 classes and 41 A's. Maybe I got smarter as I got older.

My Senior Year

While driving back to Sterling from Pittsburgh in my senior year, I was excited because this was my last year, and it was going to be great. The defense had committed to coming back bigger, and I was at 185 lbs. after working on the railroad all summer. My job was laying ties and rails and spiking them down with a 16 lb. sledgehammer, eight to ten hours a day. I was eight miles from school when I was pulled over by a highway patrolman. When the officer got to the driver's side, he noticed who I was, because I was well-known in Sterling due to my skills in football and baseball. He said, "Scales, where are you going in this car?"

I was driving a 1967 candy apple red Buick LeSabre, with a white convertible top, black leather seats, gangster whitewall tires, and an ornament on the hood. The ornament was a lady with big breasts sticking out. Plus, I was wearing a hat that had a band of mirrors around the brim. I also had a nice lean going on.

The officer asked me how the team would do this year, and I said I thought we would do well. He said that this car was going to get me in trouble, and he smiled and walked away. He was right. The year did not start as planned; the first thing to happen was that my girlfriend (the young lady from Jamaica) and I broke up. I did love Carrell, but we had nothing in common. She did not like classical music and didn't believe in my dream, plus we didn't get along very well. So instead of dragging the relationship out, we just ended our relationship, and we both went our own ways. I did not date anyone until after homecoming.

It was now our last homecoming game, and it was against our rival, Friends University. Ike and I just got back from lunch and walked into our room, which had the door open because of homecoming, and we saw this pretty young lady sitting at our card table. (Spades, anyone?) Ike asked, "Are you looking for someone?"

And she said, "Yeah, Phil Scales."

Ike turned and left the room.

I had seen her around campus but had never spoken to her. Her name was Maggie, and I had never met anyone like her before. She asked me if I played football, and I said yes.

Maggie replied, "Well, you don't look like a football player."

So, I invited her to the game. We talked for two hours, and I found out that she was a freshman and was from Aurora, CO, but was leaving at the end of the first semester because of chapel violations. Sterling required chapel on Mondays, Wednesdays, and Fridays, and if you were not in your assigned seat, then you would be marked absent. Four absences and you were kicked out of Sterling; Maggie had eight.

She said, I heard you used to date the girl from Jamaica, and I said that I did, but we were no longer together. I asked her again to come to see the game, but she said she was not sure if she would do that. As the game started, I found myself doing something that I never did, I investigated the stands. We had the number one defense, and Friends had the number two defense in the conference. The final score was Friends 35, Sterling 34, and no fights. Both teams' offenses ran up and down the field, and it was the last team with the ball that won (fun game).

I walked out of the dressing room with Ike, Stan, and Gary, but we all had little to say. As I stepped out of the locker room, I saw Maggie standing there, and I asked her if she enjoyed the game, and she said, "I thought you were supposed to win the Homecoming Game."

As I said, I had never met anyone quite like her before. So, I asked her if she was going to the musical production later in the evening.

Homecoming was always the best day of the year for me because I got to do two of my favorite things, football, and music. The two biggest things for homecoming were the big game and the musical. It was so rewarding for me to play the big game and then play my violin or viola in the pit orchestra. Over the years, we had done My Fair Lady, Hello Dolly, and Camelot, and this year we were performing Fiddler on the Roof. We had already done two performances, and this was the last one. She said she had heard that it was rather good and asked what time I would pick her up. I replied that the baton dropped at 8:00, so I would pick her up at 7:30.

I picked her up at the dorm, and she was dressed to kill. I was in my tuxedo, so as a couple we looked great, even though we were not a "couple." The performance was outstanding that night and we received two standing ovations. It was after ten, so Maggie, being a freshman, had to be back at the girl's dorm. We talked the whole way back, and when we got to the dorm, I said good night and started to walk away.

Maggie said, "You know, Scales, that was your best game of the year, and tonight's performance was the best of the three."

I replied, "I thought you said that you did not go to the games?"

She smiled and said, "Scales, you are so naïve."

For the next four weeks, we spent a lot of time together. The first semester of my senior year was ending, and I planned to leave early in the morning to head back to Pittsburgh for Christmas. As much as I was excited to see my family, the night before my departure was sad because I had to say goodbye to two dear people, Ike, and Maggie. Ike's goal was to make it into the NFL, and after four years of football at Sterling, he was calling it quits. (Ike signed as a free agent with The Atlanta Falcons a year after Bay Lawrence). Maggie was also leaving in the morning and called me from her job at the local nursing home to come to pick her up. It was 9:00 pm, and she had to go back to her dorm, but she refused, and we ended up driving down to the lake. We stayed there for over two hours, and I finally took her back to her dorm, said goodbye, and went back to my dorm.

When I got to my room, I saw two policemen standing in the middle of the room with the Dean of Men, and they were questioning Ike about my whereabouts because Maggie was 2 hours late. Ike was glad to see me because they had been questioning him for quite a while. I told them that she was at her dorm, and they called over to check on my story.

Four o'clock the next morning, I was on the road to Pittsburgh, riding back with some friends, and it was hard saying goodbye to Ike Brown. We had grown close over the years, and he would always be my brother. I got home around 5:00 pm, and at six, I had a call from the Dean of Men. He said that Maggie had left her purse in my car, so I told him that my car was on campus and unlocked. He called back a little while later and said that they could not find it and asked if I had taken the purse with me. I told him that I did not take it, nor did I know where her purse was. The Dean told me that my actions were unacceptable for a Sterling College student and that we would talk when I got back to campus.

Maggie later found her purse; she had left it at work that night. What the Dean did not know was that as soon as I got back to school, I had a 4-week student teaching assignment in Albuquerque, New Mexico, teaching at Menaul High School. This was an Independent High School where minority students (mostly Native Americans) stayed in dorms and lived on campus. This was a great experience for me, and it reinforced the other teaching block that I had during my first semester in Lyons, Kansas. When I returned to Sterling, I discovered that the Dean of Men had blocked me from attending any class until I came and saw him. I went to his office, and he informed me that he was taking all my scholarships and my dorm leadership job.

I was dumbfounded as I had no one to turn to for help, and I never told my parents that I needed money to finish college. I would be the first in my family to graduate from college, and disappointing my family was not an option. Later that night, I got a call from Maggie, and when I told her what had happened, she broke down in tears, because she knew how badly I wanted this. I took a job in Hutchinson (20 miles away) at a Cessna airplane plant, degreasing airplane parts on the third shift. I worked from 11 pm to 7 am and then would drive back to campus for my 7:45 am class. With classes all day and baseball until 5:45, I was left with only 4 hours to study and sleep before I had to go back to work. The one thing that helped me in this strenuous period was Maggie. She called every other night and sent perfume-sealed letters to my mailbox every day. You could smell the letters down the hallway, and the guys would tease me that they could smell another letter. I kept this grueling schedule for three months.

One night while in a hurry to get to work, I left my stereo on and

Earth, Wind, and Fire played all night. When I got back to the dorm, there was a note on my door from the Dean of Men that said I needed to come and see him before I went to any class. I went to his office, and he said that I had to turn my speakers in for sixty days. I protested that this was not fair, and he said that he did not care. So, now I was working the third shift at Cessna, and I had a cool stereo set with no speakers. The year was not going as planned.

The baseball team was headed out west to play St. Mary's of the Plains. This would be my last game as a Sterling Warrior. There were now two Black players on the team. Earl was a junior college transfer student, and he played football also (Wide-out). This was our last game, and all I wanted to do was hit the ball. I was the leadoff batter, and Earl was the third base coach. I had faced this pitcher before (right-hander), and he had a twin brother who was also a pitcher (left-handed). On the first pitch, I blasted the ball over the left fielder's head and Earl had me slide into third. The second time up, we got the same result; Earl had me slide into third again, and this time he pulled me and started slapping the dirt off me. Earl was more excited than I. My third time at bat, they changed the pitcher, and the other twin came to the mound (left-hander), and I blasted one off the right-field wall for another triple. I ended my baseball career with three triples and a walk. My last time up, they gave me a free walk to first base.

I had a couple of bright spots in May. I won Senior Athlete of the Year, and I signed a teaching contract in Hutchinson, Kansas. My parents were coming to my graduation on May 10, 1974. I had called the motel (in Lyons, KS, eight miles away) in November to plan for three rooms. I called the motel every month to make sure I was locked into the rooms. On May 8, my Dad, Mom, brothers (Henry and Bus), sister-in-law Lynn, and my big sister, Angie), arrived in my Dad's Cadillac Coupe de Ville. I took them to the motel and asked for my family's rooms. The lady looked at me and said that I did not have a reservation there. I tried to explain that I had called her every month to confirm, but she was not listening, so Dad said, "Let's go somewhere else."

We tried two more motels with no luck. As we walked from the third motel, Bus turned to me and asked, "You stayed out here for 4 years?"

My family stayed in the dorm that night, and Bus stayed with me. The next morning, I took my family to Hutchinson for rooms.

On May 10, 1974, I graduated from Sterling College, and out of the 45 black athletes that hit the campus of Sterling in the summer of 1970, only two were on stage, Stan (my roommate) and me. Mom and Dad were so proud, as was the rest of my family. Buster was still in college and was in no hurry to get out because he was having way too much fun. The next day, we headed for Pittsburgh, and I was driving a new car. I had traded my Buick in for a brand-new green Vega; I was an adult now. As we drove back home, Dad in the Caddy and me and Bus in the Vega, I thought about the goals that I had set for myself. I finished college in four years with a music major, won Senior Athlete of the year (the trophy went to Mom), and accepted a teaching position. I also thought about Carell and Maggie. Carell did not graduate with our class, and I wondered if I would ever see her again. As for Maggie, I believe I would not have made it those last few months without her love and support. I hoped that I would see her again, but all-in-all life was good, and Bus and I rode back to Pittsburgh, singing along the way to Joni Mitchell's "Help Me." This was Buster's favorite song, but I was the only one who knew it.

Chapter Three
Hutchinson, Kansas

I signed my teaching contract in April before I graduated. One day I got a call from Bill Lilly, and I had no idea who he was, but it turned out that he was the Superintendent of Music for the Hutchinson Public Schools, and they had a junior high orchestra position opening that summer. Mr. Lilly said that he had heard some great things about me and asked if I could come in for an interview. So, I went in the next day to talk to him. Hutchinson was a town of 52,000 people and about 8% Black. They had 12-grade schools, three junior highs, and one large high school. In the whole school district, they had two Black women and no Black men as teachers. I would be the first Black male hired in the district, but by September, they had hired another Black male and woman who came as a couple. I would be teaching at Central Jr. High, and I would also be coaching 8th-grade football. I accepted the position, and my first--year salary was $6,000. Mr. Lilly was honest with me and said there were racial tensions sometimes in Hutchinson, and that I should look for an apartment on 15th street and below, because that is where the minorities lived. The biggest phrase going around the country was affirmative action, and I knew that I probably got hired because of it. I drove back to Hutchinson and began looking for my first apartment around 26th street and above, but after 3 full days of looking, I finally ended up staying with a friend on 12th street. We had our first teacher's meeting, and I had the chance to meet Bill Garry and Vanessa Bean (the other two new Black teachers). I was kind of the talk of the town because I was the first black orchestra teacher and coach in the state of Kansas.

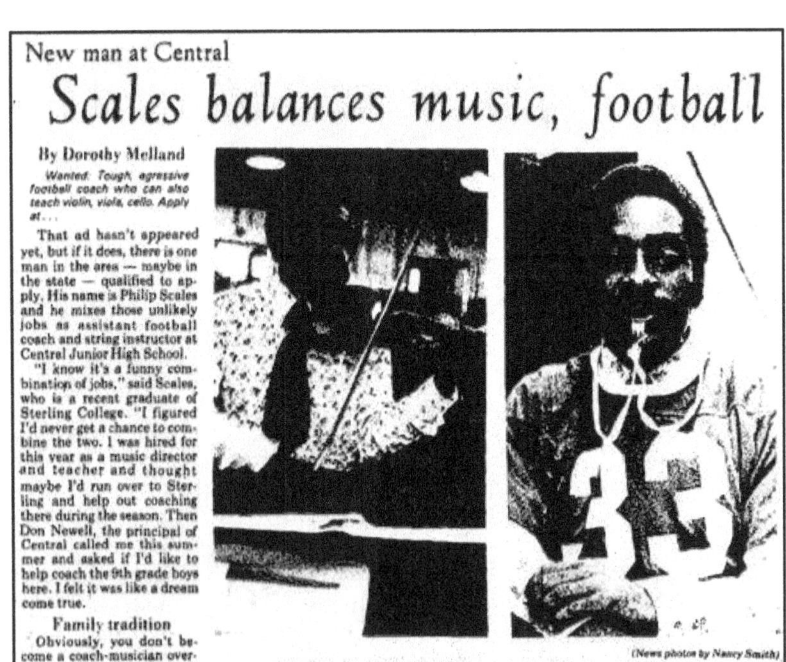

New man at Central

Scales balances music, football

By Dorothy Melland

Wanted: Tough, agressive football coach who can also teach violin, viola, cello. Apply at . . .

That ad hasn't appeared yet, but if it does, there is one man in the area — maybe in the state — qualified to apply. His name is Philip Scales and he mixes those unlikely jobs as assistant football coach and string instructor at Central Junior High School.

"I know it's a funny combination of jobs," said Scales, who is a recent graduate of Sterling College. "I figured I'd never get a chance to combine the two. I was hired for this year as a music director and teacher and thought maybe I'd run over to Sterling and help out coaching there during the season. Then Don Newell, the principal of Central called me this summer and asked if I'd like to help coach the 9th grade boys here. I felt it was like a dream come true.

Family tradition

Obviously, you don't become a coach-musician overnight. In Scales' case, it all began in third grade in his

(News photos by Nancy Smith)

PHIL SCALES ... Athletic musician? Musical coach?

I learned very quickly that college doesn't prepare you for everything that you will encounter. The first thing that they do not teach you is how to recruit your music students. I went to the other teachers to get some pointers, but their method bored me, so I knew that it would also bore the kids. My method was a high-energy style of approach, where I would play little fun tunes that they all knew. I would also let the kids hold, touch, and play the instruments that I was introducing. The whole recruiting session was about having fun while we learned to play the instrument. The two things that I have always promised my students are that they will have fun and they will learn to be good players. I started recruiting twice as many students as any other music teacher in the district.

The second thing that they don't teach you in college is how to maintain control of your classroom. Most college graduates finish their student teaching with a false sense of success, but the students that you just spent six weeks or a semester with were not really your students. The classroom teacher probably told them if they were not on their best behavior that they would drop their grade, but they are not your students. I had a couple of 9th-grade students who knew how to push my buttons, and they did for a couple of weeks. One day a 9th-grade student got the best of me, and I took her into my office and went off on this young lady.

When I was done, she calmly said, "You know, you really should learn to control your temper."

I looked at her and calmly said, "You are right. Thank you, Cordy Brown."

Five years later, I took a group to an overnight music festival in

Oklahoma, and Cordy Brown was the first chaperone I chose. I finally started having more control over the class when the students understood that the classroom rules were the same for everyone. I did not have to enforce them, but as my student, you had to follow them. I felt good about how things were going, and then on Friday, I had two boys stay after school because they had been late for class for the third time.

After school, John came into my office, and I told him that he could take a swat with a paddle and go home or stay until 4:00. (swatting was acceptable in '74). John took the swat, and it got his attention. Jimmy came in, and I gave him the same choice. Jimmy said he didn't think he wanted a swat from me, and then asked John if it hurt. John said, no, and Jimmy said, "You probably hit like a little girl."

He then bent over and touched his toes, and I gave him the same swat that I gave John. The swat was a little more than Jimmy expected, and he let out a swear word. I told the boys that I hoped that I would never have to do that again and I'd see them in class on Monday.

On Monday morning, I was called into the principal's office, joined by John and Jimmy. The two boys looked a little confused in the principal's office because they already had their punishment on Friday. The principal then asked the two boys if they believed that I gave them a swat because they were white. I was stunned by the question, but Jimmy answered no before I could say anything. Then Jimmy asked if Mr. Scales was in trouble for paddling him. The principal answered that it could be a possibility. Jimmy said good, because I got two swats from the PE teacher and one from the history teacher last week, so they should be in here also. We were all excused, and I never had a problem with Jimmy again, and I never paddled another student.

A couple of days later, I was called down to the office, wondering what was up now. I asked the secretary what she needed, and she replied that there was someone here to see me. I turned around, and it was Maggie. I also noticed that she had luggage with her. Since December, I had not seen Maggie, but we talked every other night in the summer, and the letters never stopped. Mom once told me to tell my lady friend to ease up on the perfume in the notes. I gave Maggie my door key and car keys and told her to pick me up at noon. She stayed a few days, and it was nice to see her.

After two months of teaching, I taught my students three words that would help them in class and in their daily lives. The three words were

Improvise, Adapt, and Overcome. When you come to class and need something, do not raise your hand to interrupt the class or me; *improvise, adapt, and overcome* your problem. You have a problem, so adjust to it, then do something to solve it yourself. After the students got used to me saying this, they began to use it, which saved a ton of class time. My coaching was also going great, and I had a great relationship with my players.

Shortly after the school year started, I took a part-time job as a waiter at Prairie Dunes Country Club (a $6,000 teaching contract only stretched so far.) The Country Club had a beautiful golf course, and they would host the Senior Pro Tour and the Ladies Tour from time to time, but Black people were not allowed to play the course. I had no problem with this because I did not play golf at this time in my life.

Maggie and I had grown close, and we were at the point where we had to decide if we would continue down this road. Maggie's parents were divorced, her dad was a vice principal, and her mom was a teacher. I had now made many trips to Aurora, CO, and had met both of her parents. I could still remember the pain of my first interracial dating experience. I was a man now, though, and I don't think either of us knew what to do. I needed time to clear my head, and I had a little extra money for Christmas, so I bought a single ticket to Hawaii for my Christmas vacation.

The Call that Changed My Life

The call came in November of '74, and it was Carell calling from Kingston, Jamaica. She was teaching at a boarding school and had been assaulted by a student and was in the hospital. She asked if there was any way I could come and see her. So, I canceled my trip to Hawaii and bought a ticket to Kingston, Jamaica. I thought it would still be a great trip, lying out on the beautiful beaches. I never knew that Kingston was like a third-world country, but it was. I never went to the beach but hung out in many clubs, and I found out that reggae music was not my cup of tea. I stayed for two weeks and wished that Carell was not living so far away. I felt conflicted – I did love her, but we truly had so little in common. She didn't like sports or classical music, which I was all about.

To make a long story short, when I got back to Hutchinson, I was engaged to get married in Miami in July of '75. I made the hard call to Maggie, who had told me not to go because it was a trap (I had no idea what she was talking about at the time.) She said she was sad to hear this news but wished me nothing but happiness. I would see her one more time in my life. I did not see Carell again until 2 days before the wedding. I was in Miami three days before the wedding, and I stayed with the best man, Ike Brown. Ike now lived in Fort Lauderdale, which was about 20 miles from Miami. I was glad that Ike was my best man because by being my roommate and teammate, I was always able to draw a sense of calm with him by my side. I left Ike's house about an hour before the wedding, and the plan was that I would pick up my parents and then meet Ike at the wedding. On the way to pick up my parents, I got lost in Miami and arrived at my wedding an hour late, which was not a good start. Carell's mother and aunt were quite angry with my parents and me. Dad started to get a little upset, but the wedding ended on a calmer note.

For the next couple of days, we spent time at Disney World before going back to Kansas. Carell told me that she did not have a green card during the ride back, and I asked her what that meant. She said that she had to leave the country in 30 days. She left Kansas in August of 1975, and I worked with my Senator in Kansas to get her back in the United States, which happened in May of 1976. This was not a good start to our marriage, but we were finally together.

The beginning of my second year did not get off to a good start. My office was above the cafeteria, next to the band room, and my rehearsal place was on the stage next to the cafeteria. The windows in my office had a wire running through them, and the window had a lock that you would hit up, and then you could position the window any way you wanted. On this day, I was about to open the window, and one of my students called out my name. I turned to them, but I still hit the lock to open the window.

The problem was that I missed the lock and put my hand through the window. The wire in the window ripped my left thumb so badly that blood was shooting straight up in the air, and my little finger was split in half. The students started screaming, and blood was everywhere. I clapped my wrist as hard as possible to stop the blood, and I ran down the steps to the building. The first door I reached was the teachers' lounge.

Several teachers were sitting at a table (4 women and 1 male), and as calmly as I could I called the male teacher, but everyone turned around and saw all the blood. Hopkin's shouted, "Someone get some towels."

And one teacher ran over, got some towels, and started to clean the blood on the floor. After a moment of silence, Hopkins again asked for some towels and wrapped them around my hand. He then took me to his car and then to the hospital. The hospital had a hand surgeon, and he looked at my hand and asked me what class I taught. When I told him that I was a violinist he said that he did not think I would play again. He put 44 stitches inside of my thumb and 55 on the outside. I also had 18 stitches on my little finger. The next few weeks were hard on my coaching and teaching because I could not play any string instruments, and in football practice, I kept banging my hand.

I couldn't play my instrument, so I worked harder on my conducting, and this did help the students because it gave us more time to work on following the baton. My hand got better, and I can still play my instruments, but I don't have any feelings in my little finger, and I can live with that. The school year went by fast, and Carell was back in the States. In the next two years, we had two baby girls; Tashai was born in '77, and Nadia in '78.

In 1977 I went to boot camp at Fort Leonard Wood and came out as a Sp4, and I served 6 years as Military Police in the Army Reserves. The start of 1978 was smooth because I was promoted to the high school orchestra position, making me the first-ever Black high school orchestra teacher in Kansas. I also was the varsity football defensive back coach.

Over the summer Mr. Lilly hired a new graduate from Kansas University to take my place at the junior high, and her name was Martha Hanthorn. One day after a summer football practice, I went up to the central music room, and I saw a young lady kneeling and looking into the music files. She had an olive-green skirt and a plaid green and white blouse with red trim, penny loafers, and brown shoulder-length hair.

I introduced myself, and she stood up (she was a little taller than me) and said, "Hi, I'm Martha Hanthorn."

On the first day of classes at the junior high, Martha informed the students that Mr. Scales had moved to the high school, and the students began to cry; that was a tough start for her. But Martha was brilliant and had a great personality, and soon won over her students. We hit it off right away. Since I did not want her to struggle in her first year as I did, I pulled her under my wing and showed her the ropes of recruiting and some teaching skills not taught in college. Martha was a very sharp person and caught on very quickly.

I also noticed that Martha and I had a lot in common. Martha had been in town about a week and said that her family was coming down from South Dakota with her piano, and asked if I could help her dad. That Saturday, I met her family. Her dad, Melvin Hanthorn, was a big man (before a later accident and the development of Parkinson's Disease) and he had the energy of three men. He put out his hand and said in his deep voice, "Call me Mel."

Martha's mom (Eunice) was a beautiful lady, and I called her Mrs. Hanthorn. Martha had two brothers and two sisters, and they were all young kids.

I had such a fondness for Martha that I tried to set her up with single guys I knew because Hutchinson could be a lonely town. One day Martha and I talked, and I asked her what street Mr. Lilly told her to look for an apartment. She said 22nd and up, and I laughed and said, "He told me 14th and below."

A week later, Martha's landlord told her that no Black people were allowed to visit her apartment complex, and a week after that she found a different apartment.

The year started great. I was the first Black orchestra teacher in Kansas and the first Black varsity football coach in our league. When I was hired for the junior high position in '74, it was through affirmative action, and I was known as the black orchestra teacher. When I was hired as the high school orchestra conductor four years later, I was hired as Mr. Scales, the orchestra director, because of my teaching skill and not because of my skin color.

I coached varsity football, worked on the high school musical (My Fair Lady), and played the principal viola in the Hutchinson Symphony orchestra. The conductor was Gary Fletcher, who was also the high school conductor at Bethel High School (a big school rival). He and I did not get along, but he was the conductor, and I had a lot of respect for that role.

Music Contest

Spring was always the most significant part of the year for music teachers because that is when we put our teaching skills in front of the judges. It was the spring of April of 79, and this was my first high school music contest. The event was in Wichita, 80 miles south of Hutchinson. As we came off the highway, making our way to the city, we passed a massive tree that the students from Hutchinson called the Lucky Tree. All the kids were yelling out of the window, "Hey Tree, we love you, Tree!"

This was the first time I had seen this, so I thought it was cute. We got to the performance site and went to our rehearsal room. I had to go to the main office to get my packet, and this is where it became clear that there was no one in the building that looked like me.

My orchestra took the stage, and we were ready to play our two Mozart numbers in front of the three judges. The students played very well (in my opinion), and I was proud of them. When we finished, I had to go to the main office to get our scores. Walking down the hall, I saw Mr. Lilly (our music supervisor) and my co-worker Martha Hanthorn standing by the office door. Martha began walking toward me and stopped about six inches in front of my face, and said, "Your scores are not good."

I said to myself, okay, how bad can it be? The scoring was 1 to 5, with a five being the worst, and no one ever got a five. I walked into the office to check our scores and stood next to Gary Fletcher (Bethel's orchestra teacher), who was checking his school's scores. I found my school and saw the scores from the three judges, 5-5-5. I was shocked. Gary, a big man, looked down at me and said, "Those scores had nothing to do with music, and I am sorry" and walked away. I was devastated and didn't know what to say. I didn't have the heart to tell the students that we got all 5s, so I just told them that the scores were low.

As we rolled out of Wichita, the bus was quiet until we passed the big tree, and one of the students, Brenda H., shouted, "Fuck you, Tree!"

That broke the tension, and everyone laughed, and I thought to myself, thank you, Brenda. The next day I went in to see Mr. Lilly because I wanted to go to another music festival as soon as possible. We found a music festival in Oklahoma City for the next October called the Southwestern Music Festival. This would be an overnight trip, so we had to raise funds to pay for our trip. We worked extra hard for this trip, and nothing would stop us this time. This was an excellent festival, and it was a little different from the Kansas festival. After your group performed two prepared numbers, they would then take your group to another performance area for sight-reading. The sight-reading session would give a music score to the conductor first, who would then have two minutes to review it. Then the conductor had three minutes to talk the orchestra through the song without anyone playing.

Our sight-reading piece was Festique by M.L. Daniels (who was also the sight-reading judge.) The orchestra received three ones from the Festival judges and a Superior rating in sight-reading. We were highly excited, but I still feel bad for my last year's senior class because they were unfairly treated because of me.

Since eighth grade, I dreamed of becoming a symphony orchestra conductor. However, my counselors always told me that there were no black orchestra conductors and that since I was an excellent athlete, I should focus on that instead. But now, decades later, I had worked my way this far and was still on track. Being black in Kansas during this time was extremely hard. I was up for head football coach but was passed over. I had three kids now, and my enthusiasm for my dream started to get off track. The city of Hutchinson and its racism were beginning to weigh heavy on me. I had a part-time job at one of the country clubs as a waiter and bartender, where the members treated me like a servant. Also, during this time, my marriage was starting to have some problems, which were the same problems that we had in college. My wife wasn't a classical music person and never came to any of my concerts, so it became painfully apparent that my dream was not a part of her dream. I now knew that after the music contest, Kansas would not be the place where I could find my dream. I was ready for a bit of change where I could refresh my dream and make a little more money, so I moved to Austin, Texas, where I taught for a while and then got into the insurance business.

Combined Insurance

I have always loved sales, and I had my first job as a salesman selling magazines for Keystone Readers when I was in the eighth grade. My oldest brother Henry was a manager for the company, and I worked for him. I worked 10 hours a week (Tuesday, Thursday, and Saturday) and made thirty dollars a week. Henry would take his crew of four people out to the white communities, and we would knock on doors and try to sell them magazine subscriptions. I was good at interacting with people, and I sold 10-15 subscriptions a week.

One day Henry said that I should go on commission and that he would pay me seven dollars a subscription, but I asked him what if I did not sell anything, and he said that I would then make nothing. He then pointed out that in the last three weeks, I had sold 35 subscriptions, which would have made me $245, but on salary, I only made $90. I was hesitant and waited two more weeks before I went on commission. Henry was right, though, because shortly after going on commission I became one of the top salespeople, and he began teaching me how to be a manager. When I was a junior in high school, I was a manager for a different company, and the district manager let me drive the company car, a 1969 Coupe de Ville Cadillac, for my 4-man crew. I would park in the teachers' parking lot, which would upset some of them.

After I had moved to Texas, I decided to work for Combined Insurance. You had to go to Chicago for two weeks of training, and those two weeks were the most important weeks of my professional life. This is where I met the founder of the company, W. Clement Stone. Mr. Stone wrote two books, *The Success System That Never Fails* and *Success Through a Positive Mental Attitude*. W. Clement Stone was the personification of America's "self-made man." He started with less than $100 in capital and built a multi-million-dollar organization. Mr. Stone coined two slogans, "PMA" (Positive Mental Attitude) and "Do It Now."

I left Chicago with two things in hand, a book signed by W. Clement Stone and a gold coin with *activity, knowledge, know-how, PMA, and inspiration to action* inscribed on the face of the coin. That was 38 years ago, but I still carry that coin in my pants pocket every day. Mr. Stone's philosophy helped me have the knowledge and know-how to sell insurance to the farmers and ranchers in Texas. I sold a simple Sickness Income policy and Cancer policies. I found out that Texas had its issues with racial problems, but PMA (Positive Mental Attitude) and "Do it Now" kept me grounded and successful.

I became one of the top salesmen for Combined Insurance and the only Black man at the top. After a few years, I earned my way into the National Sales Manager Hall of Fame. I received a solid gold Omega watch, and the inscription on the back read: To Phil Scales from Michael P. Hester, National Sales Manager, 1st Half 1983.

My job was going very well, but my marriage was not. Carell and I divorced in 1982, and I later married Martha Hanthorn. Our friendship had deepened over the years and slowly turned into love. Interracial marriage was frowned upon in Texas during this time, and it had only been 15 years since the Supreme Court ruled in *Loving vs. Virginia* that laws banning interracial marriage violated the 14th Amendment. Still, we both went into our marriage with our eyes wide open. We both lost friends and relatives because of our marriage, but that was their loss.

I also kept up with my music in Austin and Martha and I both played in The Austin Opera Orchestra and the Austin Civic Orchestra. I also played semi-pro football for the Austin Texans. My last game was in Chicago, playing against the Chicago Fires in the summer of 1981. That was the last game ever played on the old AstroTurf; the Bears played at Illinois University that fall of '81 until the surf was turned back to sod for the Bears.

By 1985, Martha and I had two little boys, Michael and Jason, and we were homesick for our families. Martha got a call from her best friend in Watertown, South Dakota, who said she had heard that the junior high orchestra teacher planned to retire that summer. So, we decided to move to Watertown, which was Martha's hometown, so I could be in place for the open teaching position.

Chapter Four
Watertown, South Dakota

We moved our family to Watertown, South Dakota, in March 1986. It would be the perfect move because we had splurged on a moving company, and the truck pulled up at 7:00 am in front of our home to start packing our house up. They boxed everything in the place while Martha watched the two boys, and I went out to play my last 18 holes at our country club in Austin.

The moving company had everything packed by 4:00 pm, and Martha and I loaded our car, towing our second car, and headed to Dallas, which was 200 miles away. We had two cars, two boys, and a Shih Tzu. The plan was to stay overnight in a hotel and finish the trip the next day. The temperature was 72 degrees, and we were driving in summer clothes, but during the drive a horrible rainstorm hit, and it took us 5 hours to get to Dallas.

We finally arrived at 10:00 pm and stopped for dinner. Jason was 4 months old, and Michael was 19 months old and entirely off his schedule. When we checked into our hotel room, Michael started bouncing off the walls. I had to go back to the car and sneak the dog into the hotel. When I got back to my room, Martha took Michael into the bathroom so I could get some sleep, but it did not work, so we ended up back on the road at midnight. We had been on the road for 10 minutes, and Michael fell asleep. When we hit Nebraska, there were 8 inches of snow on the ground. We made it to Watertown safely (although shivering and exhausted!), and our furniture arrived two weeks later.

I was still working for Combined Insurance. The town of Watertown had roughly 20,000 people, and only two Black men (including me) lived in the city, so selling insurance in South Dakota was just like Texas. I quickly found out that it took 3 to 5 weeks to get a state insurance license in South Dakota. However, the company still wanted me to ride with a manager, Clarion Hoag, from Redfield, South Dakota. Clarion was an older gentleman and was not a particularly good salesperson.

I met Clarion at a coffee shop, and he went over how he would train me. When he was with the client, he said I should not say a word, just smile, and I said OKAY. After the first couple of calls, it was evident that Clarion would not sell anything. On our third call, the gentleman said he did not think he was interested, and Clarion started packing everything up to leave.

I then stepped in and said, "John, let me ask you something; if you had a golden goose in the basement, and every morning you went down in the basement, and rubbed the goose on the head, and he would then lay a golden egg for your family to live on, wouldn't you insure and take care of that goose?"

John replied, "Yes, I would."

I then reminded John that he was his family's golden goose, and John understood and agreed. I then told Clarion to start the paperwork, which he did, and we sold our first application. When we got back in the car, I asked Clarion if I could give the presentations for selling the policies, and he would sign the policies. He would keep all renewals, and we would split the income right down the middle. So, for the next five weeks, Clarion wrote me a $600 check each week until my license came in. My license finally arrived, and I started working the farms by myself. One day in June of '86, I got home from work and Martha told me that Mr. Art Cirulis (the junior high orchestra director) had retired. I had two weeks before the interview and just enough time to drive to Miami, Florida, to pick up my four girls, Tashai, Nadia, Tiffany, and Erin, who stayed with us for six weeks every summer.

My Girls

When Carell and I divorced in Austin, Texas, in 1982, we had joint custody of the girls. She would have them four days one week, and I would have them for three, then we would switch the following week. One day she told me that she was moving to Houston to stay with her sister. I did not like it because that made it harder for me to see my daughters, but I understood. So, her sister and brother-in-law came up to help load the truck. Once we were finished, I hugged the girls and told the oldest one (Tashai was 5 years old) that I would see her at her aunt's house on Saturday, and she said, "Daddy, we are going to Grandma's house."

I hugged her again and said, "No, baby, you are going to auntie's house."

I got a call on Friday night from Carell, and she said that they were now living in Miami with her mother. I went to my lawyer to see what I could do, since she violated our divorce decree by taking the kids out of state without my knowledge. My lawyer said I could have her arrested or change the divorce decree. I did not want to charge my girls' mother, so I agreed to revise the decree. I now had them for spring breaks and six weeks in the summer.

This would be the girls' first summer in Watertown, South Dakota. The drive from Watertown to Miami was 1,923 miles, and I drove it all by myself, which took me two days in my little brown Nissan. I picked up my daughters and headed back to South Dakota, but my first stop was at a farm near Sullivan, Indiana. My mother-in-law and Martha were both born there, and I stopped at Martha's aunt and uncle's house. Lowell and Nellie had not met the girls before, and I did not know what to expect. I drove up to the farmhouse, and Nellie came outside. I saw Lowell walk out of the barn and then go back in.

Nellie asked the girls their names and asked if they would like a cold glass of sweet tea. I heard a strange sound from the barn and turned to see a Shetland pony pulling a small cart emerge, with Lowell at the reins. He rolled up to the girls and said, "Who wants a ride?"

Lowell loved to take all the little ones on pony cart rides. The Indiana relatives are great people, and I am honored to be a part of the family. We got back to Watertown after three days on the road, and I was exhausted. These six weeks in the summer with my daughters would prove challenging for everyone as the years went on. South Dakota culture was far different from Miami culture, and I had to learn a few slang words to understand my girls, like what did *Off the Chain* even mean?

Delayed 3 hours in the Smokey Mountains

The Interview

I had been selling insurance in South Dakota for three months, and I was already the company's top salesperson. But we had moved to Watertown so that I would be in place when the junior high orchestra teacher, Mr. Cirulis, retired. After learning and embracing the philosophy of W. Clement Stone and Napoleon Hill, my motivation to achieve my dream of becoming a Symphony Orchestra Conductor was back on track. I applied for the position and got an interview. I knew that I would have a great interview because I had the knowledge, the know-how, and the inspiration to action through PMA (Positive Mental Attitude).

As I mentioned earlier, I was one of two Black men in a city of 20,000 people. There were no men of color conducting any orchestra in South Dakota. In fact, there were not many Black men in the United States conducting an all-white symphony orchestra full-time between 1985-2000. The reasoning behind that was that an all-white symphony would not follow the demands of a Black conductor because the conductor is in total control of every sound that comes out of that group. I did not worry about this as I prepared for my interview. I have always walked through life with the phrase: "Judge me by the content of my character and not by my skin color" (Martin Luther King Jr.) seared into my brain.

While I was selling insurance, I did my homework and checked out the school system. There were only 15 students in the junior high orchestra and 23 in the high school orchestra, plus there were four public and two private grade schools. I felt that I could recruit at least 16 students in each 5th-grade class (a total of 96 students) with my recruiting skills, and then when that class reached 7th grade, my retention rate should be between 40 & 45 students. So, in three years, my junior high would have over sixty students. In five, I projected that I would have over 100 students playing in the orchestra, making Watertown the largest junior high orchestra in the state.

I was standing outside the interview room, and they signaled me to come in. I stood there for a second and remembered the teaching and the phrase of W. Clement Stone - DO IT NOW. I briskly walked into the room and sat at the head of the table. 10 people were sitting around the table, including the Superintendent, Vice Superintendent, Junior High principal, the music staff from the junior and senior high schools, and Kris, who was one of the finest violin players in the area. They asked many questions, including why they should hire me. I told them that my five-year plan was to have over 100 students in four years, and in the 5th year, the group would play at the state music convention. There was silence in the room.

Then, the Junior High principal asked me if I still had any ambition of coaching football, and I replied that I would love to coach again. The interview was over, and three hours later, I got the call that I was hired for the orchestra position and the 8th-grade football team's coach (offensive coordinator). The next day I went to the junior high to meet with the principal, Dan Albertson, and he gave me a tour of the junior high music department. The band room was huge, and the chorus room was also quite large, with built-in risers. Then we walked down a long hallway between the chorus and band room to a tiny room built at the back of the school. I noticed that the room did not have heat right away, then Mr. Albertson turned the ceiling heat fan on.

Mr. Albertson said that we would have a problem if I recruited 100 students, as when they built the junior high, they forgot to create an orchestra room. I told Mr. Albertson that he had three years. The principal let me stay a while to check out my new surroundings by myself. About an hour later, a white-haired man walked into the room, stretched his hand toward me, and said, "Hi, I am Art Cirulis."

Art had started Martha on the violin in the 1960s and later taught her younger siblings. We hit it off right away. Art was 64 years old, and we were close friends for the next 30 years.

Art was from Latvia, a country on the Baltic Sea between Lithuania and Estonia and was a POW in the Second World War. Art was a warm, generous, and honest man. He asked me my plan, and I laid it out for him. He thought that was an excellent plan but felt that the problems that I would have with that many students were twofold. One was the instruments for students, because the school only had instruments for the students in grade school, but no violins for junior high students. The second problem was that instrument repairs would be a problem, because it took three to four weeks to get a broken instrument back from either of the two music stores in town.

Art asked me if I did any instrument repair, and I told him no. He told me that he could teach me to repair the instruments. So, over the next few years, Art taught me to fix bows and make and fit bridges. He also taught me how to set sound posts, repair cracks in the face of an instrument, and put a fingerboard on any instrument. I was incredibly grateful for Art's friendship and support, but he was the only one I received support from. The staff thought that I was extremely high on myself and would not be able to do the things that I said I would do, but I fooled them all.

I was still selling insurance when school started, but I was only working on Saturdays, and my one day of sales was better than most of the agents' weekly sales. My regional manager didn't like me working two jobs and told me to pick one, so I kept my insurance renewals and walked away from the insurance job. I was now ready to pursue my dream wholeheartedly.

Coaching

Eighth-grade football practice started two weeks before school, and I was extremely excited. I would be the players' first Black coach in their life, but how scary could I be at 5'6" and 175 pounds? (short answer - very). I was a hands-on coach, which meant I would jump into any position and show the player what I wanted - linemen, running backs, and receivers. I ran a 4.6 forty-yard dash, so I was faster than most of the players. My enthusiasm, energy, and passion for the game turned my players on. The focus that we always had for our team was "teamwork." We would win or lose together.

I always felt that music and sports required the same mindset. In sports, all the players are at different levels of playing the game, and it is up to the coach to mold all those skills and abilities into a winning mindset and try to be successful on the field. Music is the same because the music students have different playing levels. My job as their conductor was to motivate and move those different skill levels forward together. There were no orchestra students playing football, and the 8th-grade football team went undefeated, 8-0. Looking back, the only thing better than coaching an undefeated team is playing on one. My Little League-Kiwanis team when I was 11 years old had a 25-0 record, and I have never forgotten how good that felt.

Recruiting

The school year started with me being the first and only Black teacher at Watertown Junior High. Most of the teachers did not understand the combination of a violin player and a football coach, let alone a Black man. I met my orchestra students, all 13 of them. They thought a music teacher named Mr. Scales was excellent. I had one class at Watertown Junior High because they put all the orchestra students in one class, and then I spent the rest of the time in the grade schools.

My first day with the orchestra was about class rules and my expectations of the group. One of the things that shocked the class was my video grading because no one had ever done it before. Many instrumental teachers will tape their students and then grade them after listening to the tape. The problem with that is if you are only listening to a tape, you cannot watch the student play and offer feedback to help improve their playing. But if I videotape a student, I can see why they are not getting a good sound, like not bowing correctly. I can also watch the tape to see if the left wrist is bent or if the violin scroll is not parallel to the floor. This method allowed me to bring a student into my office, watch the video with them, and point out what can help them improve. I introduced this teaching technique to the music staff. Some liked it, others did not, but everyone was using the technique after a year. I explained to my students that our concerts were their "final test" of their knowledge of the music that we would be working on in class.

One student raised his hand and asked if students were required to come to the concerts, and I said, "No, but the next day that you are in school, I will have the video set up for you. Since it is our big test, you will have to play the whole concert by yourself while being taped."

The students did not think that was fair, so I asked them what happened in other classrooms when they missed a test, and they said they would have to take the test when they got back to school. I then explained that when we performed the concert, I would tape it, and we, as a class, would watch it together the next day. After watching the whole performance, I would grade it, and that grade would be given to everyone in the class, because music is a team effort. The kids got it, and no one ever missed a concert.

I could take students out of class in junior high to give them lessons. In the beginning, this was not a problem, as there were so few students in orchestra, but the staff did hear about my goal to have 100 students in junior high, and that frightened them. The band teacher (Sharon) was not excited about my plans because if I achieved them, then it would put some hardship on her program, and she did not want that.

Sharon was hired by the Watertown School District in 1961 and was the junior high band director there until her retirement in 1998. She was going through a divorce, and the last thing she needed was a whirlwind of a person such as myself, which I understood.

The chorus teacher, Mary, and I were the same age. She was incredible, and we got along great and shared an office together. Still, she was different when she was around the other music people. I started my day at the junior high, and I was then off to the grade school for my first recruiting class, and I was excited. The high school teacher, Renae, and I would go into the 5th-grade rooms together, and she would talk about the cello and bass, and I would introduce the violin and viola. Renae was also my age (34), and this was also her first teaching job out of college. She had been at the high school for 12 years, but only had 25 students in the high school orchestra.

She asked me how I approached recruiting, and I told her that I was always high-energy around the students and would always try to motivate them. I said that I promised my students two things: that they will get better, and they will have fun. Renae started with the cello, then the bass, and went on to explain how the instrument produced the sound and the mechanics of the instruments. She then played a part in a beautiful cello concerto with her fingers running up and down the fingerboard. When it was my turn, with my violin in my hand, I asked who could tell me the difference between a violin and a fiddle. The kids' hands flew up in the air with answers. One said that a violin had four strings and a fiddle had five. Another proudly noted that the fiddle was 4 inches smaller than a violin. The best answer was that a fiddle was never made to play classical music.

I asked, "How many of you think this is a violin, and half of the class raised their hands. Then I asked, "how many of you believe that this is a fiddle?"

And the rest of the class raised their hands.

I raised the violin in my right hand and said, "This is a violin."

The violin people went nuts. I then put the violin in my left hand and said, "This is a fiddle."

The fiddle people went wild. I kept switching hands with the instrument saying, this is a violin, this is a fiddle. I then asked the class what I was saying, and one kid said, "When it's in your right hand, it's a violin, but in the left hand, it is a fiddle." (You've got to love kids.)

By now, the class is rolling around the floor with laughter. I told the kids that there is no difference between a violin and a fiddle; it is only a different playing style. I then played the Devil's Dream for a "fiddle piece" and for the "violin" number I played Star Wars. The students were on the ceiling, and their teacher was amazed at the kids' excitement.

After I finished playing, I told the students to go home and ask their moms and dads what the difference was between a violin and a fiddle. I told the kids that I hoped to see them next week when string classes started, and they began to clap very loudly. Renae was shocked by this response from the students and how I had just recruited them.

I used to go to a steak house named Bonanza. You could smell the steak and see these pictures of the different cuts of meat, but when you got your order, it looked nothing like the picture, even though the smell of the steak was great. I liked to walk into a classroom and "sell the sizzle and not the steak." Renae was selling the steak when she played the concerto, because it made the instrument seem complicated and not fun. The students could not envision playing like that, but they could see the fun in learning an instrument with the Star Wars and the fiddle piece. So, I always taught the fun part of the music, the sizzle. Another good example was Professor Henry Hill from the Music Man. Professor Hill sold the illusion of playing an instrument for a whole summer, using the "Think Process." Professor Hill was also selling the sizzle and not the steak.

Before leaving the room, I also told the class that I went to college on a football and baseball scholarship, plus I was coaching 8th-grade football (the guys were all in). When Renae and I stepped into the hall, she said that had never happened before. I smiled and started walking to the sixth graders' room, and Renae said we recruited them last year. I thought to myself: there is a new Sheriff in town. I recruited 110 fifth-grade students my first year, plus I went back into the 6th-grade rooms and added another 22 students along with the 10 sixth-graders that started the previous year. This meant that next year in the junior high orchestra, I would have 42 students. I returned to the junior high and went into the principal's office to tell him about the students that would be enrolled next year and that the room would be too small.

He said, "Are you making waves already, Mr. Scales?"

First week with beginners

Having many string students in the grade school quickly became a problem for the elementary teachers because I was getting tons of kids out of class at one time. Having so many students also created a space issue. A small group of students could rehearse in closets, boiler rooms, on stage, in the nurse's office, and even in the hallway (I had previously taught in all these spaces!) but having 20-25 string students in one class required more space. I tried to explain to school principals that the students deserved a quiet teaching area, just like their elementary classrooms, but it was a touchy subject.

The other problem was that some teachers would use string class as a bargaining chip and not let students come to my class if their work was not done. This was not fair to me, the student, or the rest of the class, because I only saw them twice a week, and if they got behind, then, it was hard for them to catch up. My first recruiting class in Watertown was a unique group of people, and they would do some amazing things in the next 8 years. These were my students, and I was so proud of them. The 1st year passed quickly. The 8th-grade football team went 8-0, and the junior high orchestra was moving along nicely, but the grade school string players were on fire.

I wanted to do more at the grade school level, so I organized a string music contest where students would be judged on their performance. I had over 100 string students, and I invited Brookings, Huron, and Aberdeen school districts to my music festival. This festival was the first time that all these schools had gathered to do something like this. I later also put together a junior high orchestra festival with these same schools.

All the players would get together for two days to work with a guest conductor. The first guest conductor was Larry Williams from Lawrence High School in Kansas. I had taught with Larry's brother, Bruce Williams, who was the high school orchestra conductor at Hutchinson High School when I was the junior high director. Martha had also worked with Larry when she student taught in Lawrence, and we were both excited and eager to see him again. The first festival was highly successful, and to my knowledge, this program is continuing with these schools.

First concert, May 6, 1989

The end of the school year was near, and I also wanted to start something that I had done in Hutchinson, and that was a summer strings program. I learned very quickly that the kids do not practice their instruments in the summer, so in the fall you would have to start three steps back from where they were at the end of the last school year. The problem was that Watertown did not have a summer music program, so I needed to find a solution as quickly as possible.

Summer Strings Program

Watertown had an outstanding Park & Recreation department, and they had tons of activities for the kids in the community. Still, they did not have any music activities. I approached the Superintendent for Parks & Recreation about starting a summer string program. He was hesitant because no one had done it before, and then he asked how it would be financed. I explained to him that the way I did it back in Kansas was that the department would charge a registration fee for the students, and then I would be paid 80% of the registration fee. I would run the program at the junior high and would use the music from my department. The program would run for 5 weeks, three days a week. The Superintendent thought it was a good idea but did not think many string players would sign up.

I talked to the students all year about my goals for their group. We talked about having 100 string players in junior high in three years and playing at the state music convention in four years. We even talked about auditioning for the National Music Convention in Chicago in the fifth year. Private lessons and staying active on their instrument during the summer would keep us on the road to success and help us accomplish our goals. I had three classes for the summer program in the first year. The first was a beginner's class (12 students), the second was the sixth-grade orchestra (55 students), and the third was the junior high orchestra (42 students). Every student in junior high signed up, and our first summer string program had 109 kids sign up. (My first summer string program is on YouTube under Conductor Phil Scales - 1987 Summer Orchestra).

One week before summer strings, I went to Miami to pick up the girls, and then spent the rest of June and July running the program. The first summer program was a great success, and the parents were so excited about the program. Still, I started to get a little pushback from the high school teacher because there had never been this much excitement for string instruments in Watertown. She thought that I was doing too much, too fast. Little did she know that I was just getting started.

Trouble Starts

I started my second year as a 9th-grade football coach, so I had the same players from the previous year (our undefeated team.) The players were very excited about having me again as a coach, and we started right where we left off last year. We knew that we were a good football team, and we ended the season 8-0, so this team had a 16-0 record under my coaching.

When school started, I was back in the old orchestra room, packed in with 42 students and a room full of instruments. On the first day, the principal walked into my classroom to discuss the problems that we could both see were coming. After class, he asked me how many students might be enrolled in orchestra year. I told him between 45 to 55 students could be here, with 35 returning the following year in the junior high school, so I could have possibly over 80 students in the junior high.

The room could only hold about thirty students max, but I would have to make it work for the current year. On the first day of school, I asked the high school teacher if I could have the requirements and music for the All-State Orchestra tryouts. There was a long pause, and then she asked why I would need the all-state material for high school players. I told her that I had 9th graders at the junior high, and they were considered high school students, so they were eligible to audition. She reluctantly sent me the materials, and I had four students audition for the All-State Orchestra. The students who auditioned studied violin or viola with a top violinist in the community. The cello players studied with the high school teacher because she was a cellist. All bass players studied with Mr. Nelson, who was a local professional bass player and also an extraordinary person.

Mr. Nelson lived with his mother, a retired vocal teacher for the district. There was a very tight-knit group in town that liked the string program just the way it was. This group of people always treated Art Cirulis as an outsider, and guess who got added to the list? (yours truly). Once I had the audition materials, I began my work of preparing my students for this grueling audition. The auditions started at the end of October, and the All-State concert (band, chorus, and orchestra) was the 2nd week in November. I sent 3 violin players and 1 viola student to the auditions.

The audition results were sent to the high school teacher, and she called the students who made it into the orchestra. I got to school on Monday, and my students told me that they made All-State. I asked them how they knew that, and they said that the high school teacher had called them on Saturday to congratulate them. I asked the high school teacher if she could contact me first next time because I would like to be the one to share this news with my students. This had never been a problem before because 9th graders were not allowed to audition before I arrived. The Watertown string program sent 12 students to the All-State Orchestra, which was the highest number ever.

The All-State rehearsals and concert were in Rapid City that year, and teachers all around the state were headed that way. I asked the high school teacher what time the bus would be leaving the school for the trip, and she said that I would not be going because it was a high school event. I told her that I was responsible for my 9th graders. Also,

I was a member of ASTA (American String Teachers Association), and we would be holding meetings during rehearsal time. She said that I would have to find my own way to Rapid City, 340 miles away. I talked to my principal about the situation, and two hours later, I was on the bus.

This was my first trip to All-State, and it was like my first Christmas morning. Oh, how excited I was. This was the first opportunity to meet all the other string teachers across the state, and it came as no real surprise that I was the only Black teacher at the All-State concert.

That fall the teachers at the junior high started getting a little upset about so many string students moving in and out of their classrooms. Because of my scheduled grade school string classes, I only had one class of string players at the junior high, even though the chorus and band teachers had a separate class for each grade. The other problem on the rise was the predicted shortage of string instruments, and I was trying to get ahead of that problem. The principal was very firm on the instrument problem and said that the school could not afford to buy instruments for junior high school students. So, I asked him about our commitment to always furnish instruments for the grade school kids, and he said the school district would honor that commitment. I was so glad to hear him say that because I had sixty new instruments in my inventory book. If I recruited over sixty players, then I had a huge problem ahead of me.

Instruments

In my second year back in the grade schools, I had 75 returning students from my first recruiting class. I had started 110 students last year, but the rub was that the band began recruiting in sixth grade. So quite often the string teacher would spend a year teaching the 5th graders how to count rhythms and read notes, and then the next year the parents would let their child switch to a band instrument. In the past, the string teachers would recruit 40 students, but between the dropout rate and the band starting up, that would leave the string program with maybe 15 students left, and then maybe 8 of those students would progress to junior high.

So, the fact that I had 75 returning students caught the attention of the band people. The band teachers could see that if I did this every year, they would see a significant drop in their numbers soon, but their

52

attitude was to wait and see. The principals in the grade schools were doing all they could to find my students a place to hold a rehearsal (Oops! I did it again). This second year we recruited 120 students, and it was easy this time. The string program was selling itself, because with so many students walking around the school carrying string instruments, it had become the thing to do. So, when we walked into those classrooms, we loved seeing their beaming and expectant faces.

The high school teacher started the show with Pink Panther and Jaws - she was now selling the Sizzle too. While our high recruitment rate was great, the problem was that with 120 new students and only sixty instruments in the inventory, I could say, "Houston, we have a problem."

The principals in the schools kept saying that this was a good problem, but it was still a problem. The junior high did not have all the money I needed for my problem. So, I did what I always told my students – *Improvise, Adapt, and Overcome* your problem.

I only had a music budget for junior high, so I went to the grade school principals and asked for funding for the upkeep and purchase of grade school instruments. I did not think it was fair for my junior high budget to pay for elementary school instruments, strings, and other supplies (for low-income students). They all agreed that I was right, so I ended up with a budget for each school, enough to buy sixty more instruments. I had all my instruments by the end of October. The music staff could not believe I got this done, but I was just getting started. I also noticed proudly that I had just as many guys playing a string instrument as girls.

Grade School I Tour

I wanted my orchestra to be a performing group that could perform for community groups. There were so many groups in the community that would enjoy a good string group performance, like the Lions Club, Kiwanis club, nursing homes, and Ladies Auxiliary Club. I also thought a I grade school tour would be a fun idea. So, I went to my principal and laid out my plan because his approval meant that I could take the students out of school to perform. This meant the teachers could be upset with the principal instead of Phil Scales. I believe the principal thought it was a good idea but never thought the students would ever get that good. The orchestra students were excited at the thought of getting out of classes to go play in the community. The first week of November, we got our first gig, playing for the Kiwanis Club, thanks to my father-in-law Mel Hanthorn, who was a Kiwanis Club member. He had a group of friends that came over to his garage early every morning for coffee and hung around until noon. One day Mel asked, "Are those kids ready yet?"

And I responded that we were just waiting for a call. The next day the principal walked into my office with a note to call the Kiwanis Club. I did, and they asked if my group could play for their morning breakfast (Thank you, Mel). I had forty-two students get out of school at 9:30 to load our bus, and we were back by 11:15, but the teachers were unhappy. The orchestra did a great job, and the Kiwanis members gave the kids a standing ovation. Mel gave a quick wink.

The performance at breakfast let me know that we were ready for my next project, the grade school tour. My grade school I tour idea would involve all six grade schools. My junior high students would load the buses at 8:15, and the first performance would be at 9:00 in the first-grade school gym, with all the elementary students sitting on the floor. The program was a mixture of I music and fun selections that the students would like, such as the "Addams Family" theme. When we performed this song, I had the players in the back of the orchestra put gloves on their bows, and as we played, they would raise the glove on the bow up and down, which reminded the audience of the single hand in the movie.

I would also involve the grade school students in the concert by selecting a student to come up and direct a song. The song I selected was *The Magnificent Seven,* and the student would come up to the podium, I would give them my baton and show him or her how to start, then I would walk away and let them do their thing. The orchestra was taught not to watch the conductor but just smile as they played. We would end the concert with a sing-along to *Rudolph the Red-Nosed Reindeer,* and I would turn to face the students and sing with them. This was a great start for next year's recruiting. The show was 30 minutes long, and then we were back on the bus to get to the next grade school. We played three concerts in the morning, then went to McDonald's for lunch. After lunch, we did three more shows and made it back to the junior high five minutes before school got out. The students were drained but were so excited about the whole day.

I was frustrated at the significant pushback I received from the faculty, who felt my students were getting out of school too much. The high school teacher and her friends believed that I was doing too much too fast and that I was starting to rock the boat, but I was just getting started. The music staff mockingly called everything I did the "Phil Scales Show." I now had 195 students in grade school and 42 in junior high, but now I had to keep up with instrument repairs. If a student broke an instrument and I took it to one of the two music stores in town, it would take at least 4 weeks to get it back, and that was valuable time that the student did not have an instrument.

I went to the principal, and asked if I could repair the instruments at a lower cost than the music stores and get the instruments back in the hands of the students in a couple of days, would I have his approval? The cost to re-hair a violin bow was 60 dollars. I would do it for 25 dollars. Fixing a crack in the face of an instrument would cost over 100 dollars, but again I could do it cheaper and faster. The principal thought it was a good idea, but I needed to send in an invoice and then a check would be issued for instrument repairs.

This worked fine until someone noticed that a check was going to Phil Scales every month for repairs. The principal called me into his office and told me that the district said they could not continue to pay me for repairs because it was a conflict of interest. I had too many instruments for my repair budget, so what could I do? *Improvise, Adapt, and Overcome*; that is what I had to do. I went to the music store where I did most of my shopping and gave them a business proposition. I floated the idea of them hiring me as a string repairman. I would bring them an invoice for instrument repairs, and they could then add anything they wanted to the bill and then send it to the school district, and once the Administration sent them a check, they could cut me a check. They added 20%, and everyone was okay with this arrangement since the check did not go directly to me, even though it cost the school district more money.

The school year was moving quickly, and I was preparing for a spring music contest with 195 elementary students playing solos, duets, trios, quartets, and large group ensembles. Plus, this year, I added the junior high students. We held the music festival at the junior high on a Saturday morning. As expected, teachers did not want students in their classrooms over the weekend, but thankfully the principal handled that issue for me. I hired all the local string teachers to be the judges and paid them, and they did a very professional job.

This was a grueling day because I wanted every student to do well, and the stress was unbearable.

There was a parent there whose daughter was one of my grade school players. She could see that I was eating my heart out over my students, so she reached into her purse and gave me a pack of roll-aids, and she would continue to do this for the next eight years. The school year was running out, and I reminded the grade school players that the Summer Orchestra registration sign-up would be out soon, and that it was a lot of fun. The school year ended on a solid note.

My summer orchestra enrollment had 15 beginners, 75-grade school strings, and 75 junior high students. The junior high vocal teacher decided to join in on the fun and had over 40 students sign up this summer. The summer looked exciting, and as usual, I headed first to Miami to pick up the girls before summer classes began.

Summer Football Camp

Watertown was a sports town, and football and basketball were the weekend entertainment. If you went to a Friday night game, you would have to get there almost two hours before the game to get a seat, and the same was true for basketball. The head football coach always ran a summer camp, which involved all the coaches, and this year we had a special guest, Rich Gannon. Rich was the quarterback for the Minnesota Vikings, and he was my mother-in-law's favorite player. He was also from Philadelphia, so I was very excited to work with him and talk about the Steelers and the Eagles. When I got a chance to speak one-on-one with him, I asked him for an autograph for Mom. Rich wrote: "To Eunice, Best Wishes, Rich Gannon #16." On our lunch break, I ran the note over to Mom's house, and she was so excited. That night Mom called me over to the house and thanked me by baking my favorite coconut cream pie.

The summer was just about over, and had been very busy between family activities, music classes, and summer football. I realized I had a big decision facing me. My orchestra students were highly motivated to improve and work toward our goals, and I had many grade school and junior high students who wanted private lessons and wanted to take them from me. But my time after school was taken up by football practice with two and a- half-hour practices. I needed to be accessible to my music students, so I quit coaching football. I always said that my athletic ability got me into college, but my musical ability would get me into society. That is where I was now, so I needed to make this decision for the good of my students and the program.

Chapter Five
The Call

This was my third summer in Watertown, it was the third week of July, and the summer had flown by. The girls had a great summer, and we celebrated Michael's third birthday. We also bought a house, and on this hot summer day, we spent all day working on this house. I went to bed utterly exhausted, and at 3:00 in the morning, the phone rang. I thought that this could not be good news, and it was not. I heard my oldest brother Henry's voice, and he said that Dad had suffered a stroke and a heart attack. I said I was on my way, and I heard him say, Phil, please hurry.

We now had a massive problem because the girls were going back to Miami in four days. We had to decide whether to take them with us and then drive to Miami from Pittsburgh or leave the kids with Mom and Mel and drive back to get them. We decided to take all of them with us. The problem was that we had to wash and pack all their clothes, and I wanted to be on the road in two hours. Martha ran across the street to Rick & Julie's house at three in the morning. Rick & Julie had graduated from high school with Martha and were great neighbors. Martha explained the situation and asked if she could use Julie's washing machine to get on the road quicker, as no laundromats were open. Julie said it was no problem, and Martha went back and forth between our house and Julie's, managing the laundry situation. When she was returning to the house, our neighbors next to us (Ken & Rhonda) asked if there was a problem, and we explained the situation about my dad. Rhonda insisted that they help too.

With the help of our good neighbors, I was on the road by 5:00 a.m. The drive from Watertown to Pittsburgh was 22 hours, and I drove every bit of it. This was 1988, and we did not have a cell phone, so I had to stop every few hours to call home to see how Dad was doing. I drove through the worst fog ever in Ohio at midnight. I could not see, and I was afraid to stop because someone might run into me, so we plodded along the highway in the fog until we ran into Pittsburgh. I parked the car in the hospital parking lot around 1:15 in the morning and left Martha and the kids in the car. It took me 20 minutes to persuade the nurse at the desk to let me see my dad.

The family is growing

I talked to Dad while he lay there in a coma. We got to my parents' house around 2:30, and Mom was still up waiting for us. Dad passed three days later, and he had the longest funeral procession I ever saw; 88 cars drove to the cemetery. The next day I was on the road to Miami to take the girls home. I dropped the girls off and started our trip back home (2,000 miles). When we got back to Watertown, the first thing I did was to write my letter of registration to the head football coach.

String Instrument Invasion

The problem had finally arrived; I had 85 string students in the junior high, and the room was too small. I got a kick out of watching all the string players walking into the junior high with their instruments on the first day of school. It was an invasion of string players, and even the teachers could not stop talking about them. The principal got the music staff together to see what needed to be worked out with space. I was still running one class at the junior high, so I was given the second period for my class, and it would be in the vocal room. The vocal room had built-in risers, so I could get all the students to fit in the space. I told the principal that this would work this year, but when I went over the 100-student mark next year, we would need to break the orchestra students into their class groups because it takes longer to tune string instruments than the band. Tuning would take up all the class time.

A Black Man's Adjustments

I had been in Watertown for 2 ½ years, and I'd tried extremely hard to fit into the community. My family attended the First United Methodist Church, the same church that Martha grew up in. I was a Sunday school teacher, children's choir director, and high school choir director. I also played in church league basketball and co-ed volleyball in my spare time. I played viola in the Brookings Symphony, under the direction of John Colson at South Dakota State University, and I also played at Northern University, in Aberdeen. Apart from that, I also started working on my master's degree at South Dakota State University in Brookings.

There were times when I almost completely forgot that I was a black man until I was walking down the street and someone would say, "Hi, Mr. Davis, my mom loves the table that you built for her."

Mr. Davis (the only other Black man in town) was the woodshop teacher, and he made furniture in his spare time. There would be times when Mr. Davis would be out with his family (two boys and a girl), and someone would approach him and say, "Mr. Scales, we loved that concert last night."

And Mr. Davis would say, "Well, I will tell him when I see him."

Mr. Davis's son's first name was Philip, the same as mine. Philip was a good track star, and he was getting scholarships from all over. They would send them to the administration office, and they, in turn, would send them over to the junior high and place them in my mailbox. I asked the secretary why Philip Davis's mail was in Philip Scales' mailbox, and she said, "Well, I'm sure you will see Mr. Davis later, so just give it to his son."

I told her that Robert and I did not hang out. She said, "Oh, I thought you two would be together all the time."

I was immersed in the community going about my business, but now and again, racism would raise its ugly head. I was once in a heated discussion with a teacher, and she said that she could not be prejudiced because she sold her home to a Black man (Mr. Davis). Many of the teachers at Watertown Junior High went to that junior high as a student, went on to one of the state universities, and then came back to Watertown to teach. There were very few minorities in the colleges in South Dakota, so a high percentage of the teachers had never encountered a Black man.

When I look at my education, I can honestly say that I never had a Black teacher. So, all my students faced something that even their teachers had never encountered - a Black teacher. I took my role as an educator seriously. I tried to be a good role model, and when it was Black History week, I would give a speech to the whole student body (1,200 students) about famous Black people. I would ask the students who was the spark for the civil rights movement. The hands would fly up, and they would shout out two names, Rosa Parks, and Martin Luther King Jr. I would then say, would you believe me if I told you that it was a 14-year-old boy?

The young Black kid's name was Emmett Till. I had been telling the Emmett Till story to my students since 1974, when I first started to teach. After Emmett's story, I would then ask who was the first lady to refuse to give up their seat on a bus. Hands would go flying in the air again, and the name that came out was Rosa Parks. I looked around the room, and I could see the teachers smiling because they thought they knew the answer. The teachers' smiles turned to frowns when I told them that the first person to refuse to go to the back of the bus was Claudette Colvin. She refused to move or give up her seat, so the police dragged her, fighting and crying, to the police car. The President and Secretary of the NAACP went to the police station to talk to Claudette to see if she was the case they wanted to pursue and get the church-going people involved. Claudette, however, was a young pregnant teen, and the NAACP did not think that church-going Black people would rally around an unwed teenager. Hence, they paid her fine and waited for another day.

I then asked the students who, in October of 1955, refused to give up their seat on the bus, and their answer again was Rosa Parks. The teachers were smiling again, but not when I told the students they were wrong again. In October 1955, eighteen-year-old Mary Louise Smith refused to give her seat up to a white woman, and she was arrested. The NAACP President and Secretary went to talk to Mary Louise Smith to see if she would be a suitable case that would spur church-going people to get out and protest on her behalf. Mary Louise would have been a great case, except her father was a known alcoholic, so they paid her nine-dollar fine and continued to wait for the right person.

I then said to the students, "In December 1955, a person refused to go to the back of the bus; who was that person?"

No hands went up, not even one, but there was one little voice that quietly said, "Rosa Parks?"

And this time, that was the right answer. Rosa Parks was arrested for not giving up her seat and was taken to jail. The President of the NAACP knew that this was the proper case because Rosa Parks was the Secretary of the NAACP, and her background was impeccable. Rosa had a run-in with this bus driver before and was intimately involved in the other two cases. The president of the NAACP then called Martin Luther King Jr., the 26-year-old new pastor of Dexter Avenue Baptist Church, and said excitedly, "We got it! We got our case!"

The teachers were beside themselves because they had never heard about this part of history before and could not believe it. I asked the students whether they thought the other two ladies should have been in the history books. They agreed that they should have been listed as the first two to refuse to move or give up their seat.

I also talked about another important Black man, Lewis Howard Latimer. He invented the carbon filament so that light bulbs could burn longer, which was the driving point of Edison's light bulb. Lewis Latimer also wrote the blueprint for Alexander Graham Bell's invention of the telephone. He installed all the lighting in New York

City and London. My favorite story was about Deputy U.S. Marshal Bass Reeves. He was appointed as the first black deputy U.S. marshal west of the Mississippi. Bass Reeves always brought his prisoners back alive, and he would have fun doing it because sometimes he would dress up to fool the criminals. He had an Indian partner that helped him out. In the early days of radio, and then later TV, they had a show about Bass Reeves, called "The Lone Ranger," but when it hit TV, Bass Reeves (The Lone Ranger) was portrayed as a white man.

These incredible stories of successful Black people were not being told in our schools, which is why I've told these stories since 1974. I felt it was essential for people to know these stories, even though there were very few blacks in South Dakota. The teachers would always question me about my stories because they had never heard of them, because they were not included in the schoolbooks, which was the point of Black History Week. The principal would always sit in the back and smile; at least I knew that he was in my corner.

A week later, one of the history teachers wanted to show the students what racism and discrimination looked and felt like. He had 45 of his 90 students bring 30-gallon black garbage bags to school, put them over their heads, and put their arms through the bag to cover their entire bodies with the black bag. They were now the "Colored People," and if they needed to use the restroom, there was one at the end of the junior high marked "Colored People Only." If they needed water, there was a water fountain at the other end of the school marked "Colored People Only." The hardest thing for me to watch was the cafeteria right outside of my room, where they had one table in the far corner marked "Colored People Only," and that's where all the garbage bag people ate. This was a three-day project, and if anyone ever felt "uncomfortable," they could take the bag off. I was the only one feeling uncomfortable, but no one asked the only Black man in the school how he felt. The students carried the project out for three days, and then discussed their feelings about the project.

One of my orchestra students, who wore the black bag for three days, came up to me and said, "Mr. Scales, I now know how you feel, and I think racism sucks."

I told John, "You have no idea how I feel because anytime you felt uncomfortable, you could just take the bag off, and at the end of the day, you would put the bag in your locker and go home. I cannot remove my skin; it has been with me all my life, so you do not know how I feel."

The next day I was called to the Superintendent's office and told if I ever talked to a student like that again, he would put a letter of reprimand in my file. The ironic thing about this is that the Superintendent had every teacher in the district post a sticker on their doors for Black History Month that read "Tolerance."

I went to my principal at the junior high and told him that I was upset with the whole project. I was surprised that none of the teachers would take the time to ask me if the project offended me as a Black man because it did, and that did not bother them. If they had asked, I would have suggested making the project short people versus tall people. The short people would do the same thing as the black garbage bag people did; the big difference in these results would be that the short people would still be short at the end of the three days. Then they would have genuine feelings of discrimination, but no one asked.

Teachers' adjustments

It was now my 3rd Christmas season at the junior high, and time again for the grade school tours, which meant that I would be getting 85 students out of classes all day to perform for the grade schools. The teachers were agitated because the orchestra had already played for the Women's Club, three nursing homes, the Lions Club, and the Kiwanis Club. We also supplied the music for the sewing class fashion show. The number of students getting out for lessons was driving them crazy.

I had told everyone that the junior high orchestra would be a performing group. Before I arrived, the orchestra concert always performed in the same concert with the choir. The choir would sing for 30 minutes, and the orchestra would play for 25 minutes, but with all the performing that the students were doing now, we had enough music prepared for a full hour just for ourselves, which meant extra rehearsal time for the students to get out of class.

I had been in Watertown for a while now, and I did not have any teacher that I could call a friend. Martha and I were not invited to any parties, and I did not even know where the teachers hung out outside of school. I did not let it worry me because we had Martha's family, and they were great to the boys and me. I was wrapped up in my work. I accepted an additional part-time teaching position at Mount Marty

College and taught four hours on Wednesday nights.
Summer of '89

I finished the school year with our String Music Festival. We had over 195 grade-school players and 85 junior high students at the festival, along with 8 judges. My summer program was off the charts, or as my Miami daughters would say, "Dad, that's off the chain."

I had over 140 students involved with the summer strings program, and it was still growing. I started getting string students that lived in other towns that did not have a string program and had students coming over 50 miles to play in my groups.

Still leading off at age 38

I also played sandlot baseball for the Watertown Merchants, and I was the oldest player on the team (38). I still had the skill to be a leadoff batter, and it was fun to play baseball again. I was the only Black person in the league, but that did not bother me. On July 4, I ran to the store to get some ice, and when I got back, Martha was sitting on our front steps, and she told me that my Grandmother had passed. My Grandmother was an extremely important person in my life. She is the only person that ever called me Philip, and we all called her Grandmother. Grandmother (my Dad was her oldest son) lived down the hill from us, and Mom would drop me off on her way to work until

I was old enough to go to kindergarten. When I was in college, I would get letters from my Grandmother, and sometimes she would put a five-dollar bill in the letter. When I was a grown man, my Grandmother would still write me letters. The last letter from Grandmother was in April of 1989. This was a sad letter because it was coming up on a year since Dad had passed (7/27/1988) and Grandmother said she did not think she could bear to be alive for that anniversary.

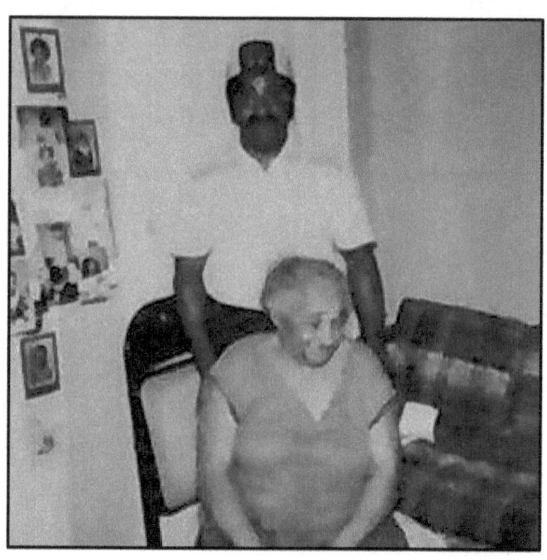

Grandmother passed on July 4, 1989, sitting in her chair with her bible and a picture of my dad in her lap. One funny story about Grandmother, she had a phobia that when you die the undertaker will take all your personal belongings after everyone has left, then bury you, so Grandmother wanted her grandsons to completely cover her grave before we left. I went with my Mom to make the arrangements for my Grandmother's funeral, and I told the undertaker that the grandsons would bury Grandmother. He assured me that would not be a problem. On the day of the funeral, Grandmother had an 80-car procession, and I was riding in the lead car with Mom. When we got to the gravesite, the undertaker came up to the lead car and told my Mom that he could not let the grandsons bury her because of his insurance. Mom said, "fine, you tell her grandsons that they cannot bury their grandmother."

The undertaker looked down at the line of cars and forty Black men emerging from the cars with shovels, and the undertaker said, "Y'all be careful, Mrs. Scales."

So, my cousins and I each told our favorite story about Grandmother and then put a shovel of dirt on the casket, and when we left, Grandmother was buried. I know she would have been proud of us.

We did not take the kids with us to Pittsburgh this time because Martha had already set up babysitting arrangements before I got back home with the ice. So, it was an easy trip, and when we got back, I finished the summer strings program and baseball, and then took the girls back to Miami.

Most important year of my life

The summer was closing fast, and I got a couple of calls before school started that would change my career. One was from Lincoln, Nebraska, and the Superintendent asked if I could direct their all-city orchestra in October. The other was from the South Dakota High School Music Activities. They asked if my junior high orchestra could perform at the State Music Convention in February 1990. I said yes to both offers.

The new school year started with a bang because we knew the numbers in the string program were coming, and now, they were here. I had 120 string students in the junior high orchestra and the principal reneged on his agreement. I felt that he had a lot of pressure from the staff over the summer and could not find a way to please everyone, so he reneged on his promise to me. The promise was that if I got 100 students in the orchestra, he would cut my class into their proper three sections (7-8-9 grade), but he did not do that, so I had 120 students in one class period.

The good thing was that I have always been able to have great discipline in my class. I was a man with very few rules, but everyone followed the rules, and that is what made us a team. I taught my students from the very beginning that you cannot excel in music without discipline, and it starts in the classroom. The students were taught that when I stepped on the podium or stood in front of them, all talking and playing stops, and if you are talking while I am talking, you would hear these words, "Pack up, please." Once you heard that, there is nothing else you can say because you are now done for the day; you do not get to leave class because you are still part of the class, but you do not get to play today. I used the same principle when we were tuning, no sound at all. I had to lean on my discipline rules with this class because it was so large, but I would not change how I taught. I tried to make my young students express their feelings through their instruments, and that takes discipline.

The students in junior high had been with me from the start, so they knew what to expect from me, and they also knew that I would fight for them. So, now I had 120 students in one class, and 25 of those violin students did not have instruments. My orchestra was filled with kids from all economic backgrounds, and the music stores were selling the instruments at an inflated price, and the families could not afford them. I went to the two stores to see if they could make any changes for the students, but their prices were set. So, I got in touch with Southwestern Strings in Tucson, Arizona, and inquired about their student violins, which were the Klaus Mueller brand. The instruments ran for $250, and I explained the problem I was having with the shortage of instruments for the kids. They told me if I bought the instruments in bulk, then they would sell each instrument to me for $200. The instruments that they were selling in Watertown were around $700 and higher.

I knew the music stores were selling better instruments, but the students could not afford their prices. I did not want my students to go out at this stage and spend a lot of money on an instrument because it would still sound the same because of the student's playing ability. Once the student had learned vibrato, shifting, and bow control, they could then go out and find the instrument suited for them, which would be in high school. I asked the rep from Southwestern Strings how much he would charge me for 40 instruments, and he said that we could make a deal for $8,000.

I waited until that evening when I had a chance to talk this over with Martha. She was currently the band teacher in Castlewood (25 miles away) and pregnant with our third son. She understood my commitment to my students and building the string program. The next day I took my lunch break and went to the bank to borrow $8,000. I secured the loan, called Southwestern, and ordered 40 violins and violas (cello & bass players could rent from the school until they graduated).

I received all my instruments in three days, and I had them sent to my house. I told the kids that needed an instrument to have their parents call me at home. The parents called, and I told them the price was $200 and they could pay me what they could when they could. I paid all the taxes, and the parents were grateful for my thinking of their child. I stood in front of my orchestra five days later, and every kid had an instrument, and we were ready to get started.

Then all hell broke loose because it had gotten out into the community that Phil Scales was selling instruments to his students and not letting them buy from the local stores (which was so far from the truth). I was called again into the Superintendent's office and questioned about selling the instruments. I explained why I did it and he understood but said that this would be the last time that this ever happened again, or I would receive a reprimand in my file (Number 2).

This was not the first time that I had bought things for my orchestra students. I had a dress code for the concerts, and it was sent home on the first day of each school year. My dress code was white shirts or blouses, black pants or skirts, and black dress shoes (no gym shoes or sportswear). I kept several white shirts and blouses on the bottom shelf in my office for any student who could not afford one. I would discreetly talk to a student who did not have a white shirt and would give them the shirt to be used for the upcoming concerts. I also got the school to buy red cummerbunds for each student.

I wanted the music to be the most important thing that was happening on stage, and not about who was wearing what. I had one student who wore his dad's black shoes to concerts because he did not own a pair. I called this *Improvise, Adapt, and Overcome* your problem. I always tried to set an example for my students, so I wore a tie every day. My students were rich, poor, good kids, bad kids, athletes, and students that had a hard time fitting in. The teachers could not understand how I could have so many students and not have a discipline problem. That was my niche with the students, treating all students the same, regardless of who their parents were.

The first goal that I had for this group was to be able to tune the whole class in 12 minutes, starting when the bell rang for the start of class. I had one of the leaders take the roll as I started to tune; if a string was broken a leader would thread the string, and then I would tune it when I got there. Since I could not get into the choir room ahead of time, I would have a leader put the assignment up on the board for the day. I had the tuning down to 10 minutes a week later. The recruiting year had started in grade school, and guess what? We picked up another 115 students. I now had to change things a little in junior high, because the teachers did not want so many kids getting out of school for all our performances, so I started a Pops string group of the top 40 students, and of course, everyone wanted to be in it.

My biggest challenge was finding the right level of music for them with all the different playing levels within the group. I always told the kids that I wanted 100% of their ability. I knew every player's ability in my group because when we did the test, it was by video, and I had a chance to sit with each student and evaluate their level of playing. I knew that everyone's 100% was different, because if Jill missed four notes out of ten, then that was Jill's 100%, and I expected six out of ten notes to be correct every time. If she believed that, then sometimes Jill might get seven out of ten notes right, which only helped the group. I worked with each student on our mission.

My group's playing in the community had paid off because my junior high had been selected to play at the State music convention in Brookings that year. My prediction had come true, and the junior high students were so excited. We took our grade school tour, and the junior high principal let me take all 120 students on the tour. We had three buses, 7th grade, 8th grade, and 9th grade. I rode with the 9th-grade bus, and I had 6 adults as chaperones, and it turned out to be a great day. When we got back to junior high, the secretary told me that I had a phone call.

Chapter Six
A Dream Come True

I called the person back and she introduced herself as the President of the Huron Symphony, and she wanted to know if I could be a guest conductor for the Huron Symphony on March 17, 1990. She said that a friend of mine had asked them to look at Phil Scales. I asked her who this friend was, and she said Art Cirulis. The rehearsals were on Monday nights and Huron was 100 miles from Watertown. This had been my goal since 8th grade, to direct a symphony orchestra, and now I had my foot in the door. I called Art to thank him, and he was excited to hear that I got the guest conductor position. I asked if there was anything that I needed to know about the group. Art said that the strings were weak and needed more cello, but he would love to come up and play for me. Every Monday night after that, Art rode shotgun with me to the Huron Symphony.

I started rehearsals for Huron the first week of the new year (1990). I noticed a couple of things right away with the orchestra. First, they were weak in the string section, but the wind section was strong. The orchestra had about 35 members, but I could bring in import players to help the sections. The orchestra played mostly arrangements of symphony pieces. I was a very picky rehearsal director because I would stop a lot to correct a section, but once we fixed the musical errors then we should never have this problem again and we could move on. After a couple of rehearsals, I started to have more players join the group, trumpets, clarinet, oboe, bassoon, and percussion players. I brought several of my students to Monday night rehearsals (violin & viola). This was a great commitment for my students because they would leave with me at 5:00 to get to the 7:00 rehearsal, and we would get back to Watertown at 11:30 that night. I had three months to prepare the Huron Symphony and I only saw them once a week to get this project done.

An Important Year

My junior high orchestra was preparing for the State Convention in February of 1990, and the timing was right in line with the five-year plan that I presented at my interview. I had predicted that I would have over 100 students in the group in five years and that we would get selected to perform at the State Music Convention. We had a solid performance prepared for the Convention, showcasing our strength in performing different styles of music. I can still remember hearing the announcer say, "Watertown Junior High Orchestra, under the direction of Phil Scales, please take the stage."

I sent 120 students on stage, dressed in white tops, black bottoms, black shoes, and red cummerbunds. Once the students were seated, I tapped my right pants pocket, which had my gold coin from W. Clement Stone in it, and walked out on the stage to face my group. As I walked out, the whole orchestra stood, which they had never done before, and I was humbled. We played music for a solid forty minutes, and the students were very poised because we had done about 14 concerts already this school year.

So, what did the other music teachers see when they watched my orchestra? Well for one, all the bows were going the same way all the time, the students were all playing in the same area of the bow, and the intonation was particularly good. The most important thing they saw was that all the students were watching me. This was the most important thing to me because my students knew that Mr. Scales could change the tempo at any time or cut everyone off at any time, so they must always watch me. Plus, I talked all the time about feeling the music and not just playing the notes, so a lot of the students moved with the music. When the performance was done, the group received a standing ovation from the audience, and they were excited.

As the students were leaving the stage a man walked up to me and introduced himself as Dennis Tischhauser. I knew about "Tish" and his band program, but I had never talked with him. Tish was like me, a band director that kept pushing the envelope for his students. He would bring 35 students to the high school music contest, and they would be entered in 110 events; his students doubled on every instrument. Tish was also a very sharp dresser like me; the suit he had on that day was the same suit that I had hanging in my closet. Tish was impressed with the numbers in the group and the performance. He became the best friend that I ever had in South Dakota; years later I would be Tish's best man at his wedding. Tish was the Phil Scales of the band world. We both respected every student and in return, we got the same respect from the students. We both talked and walked the walk, so our students always knew where we were coming from.

I had reached another goal with my students because when I recruited them, I had promised them that this day of playing at the State Music Convention would come. I also told them that after the State Convention, I would enter them in the National Convention in Chicago, which I did by sending the tape of our performance at the State level. My principal came up to me and said that he was immensely proud of the kids and the program. I never got a single word from the high school string teacher or band director from Watertown.

The Dream

I finished the State Convention, and now I had 30 days to get ready to fulfill my 8th-grade dream of conducting a symphony orchestra. I'd worked with the symphony since January, and we were coming together quite nicely. The orchestra had grown comfortable with my style of conducting, and they were gaining confidence and trust in my ability and knowledge of the music. I wanted to raise the bar for this group, and the only way I could do that was by them learning to trust me. I had some good players who had not been pushed musically in a few years, so it was a tightrope to walk, and again, this was a period where there were only a few black conductors, and I was the only one in the state of South Dakota.

The wind players were gaining a lot of confidence in me because of my knowledge of wind instruments, because I could play all the wind instruments. In college, I played the French horn in the concert band, bari sax in the jazz band, and trumpet in the pep band. I was also the only one in the woodwind section who could double tongue on the oboe. When I was teaching in Hutchinson, I worked with a band instructor named John Simpson. John was an outstanding brass teacher, and he also worked with the Hutchinson Sky Riders (drum & bugle corps). I learned so much from John, and he also let me direct one of his jazz bands in Hutchinson. John also taught me a lot about counting rhythms. I always had a saying with my students, if you cannot count it then you will not be able to play it. I used this teaching method with my wind players, and they responded very well.

On the day of the concert, we had a dress rehearsal scheduled from 3:00 to 5:00, then the players from out of town, Martha, Art, and any student that I brought with me that was playing in the orchestra would go to Huron's Barn Restaurant. The Barn was famous because Cheryl Ladd from Charlie's Angels grew up in Huron and was a waiter at the Barn when she was a teenager. The concert was at 7:30 and everyone was already on the stage. Martha, who played in the 1st violin section, kissed me for luck and told me that she was proud of me.

I stood out in the hall and said a prayer, thanking my Savior for giving me the strength and will to follow my dream. I then tapped my right pocket with my gold coin in it from W. Clement Stone and said out loud, "Do it Now."

I quickly walked out on the stage for my debut. The concert went very well, and the newspaper gave the symphony and conductor a great review; a week later the Huron Symphony Board asked if I would come in and interview for the open conductor's position. The board had a ton of questions and I answered them all. The most important question was, where do you plan to take this orchestra? I told them that I planned on raising the bar and adding many more players.

The board asked where these players would come from, and I said that I would bring in top high school students from Huron and Watertown, but the symphony would be run under adult rules, and I would also reach outside of Huron for local talent. The goal would be to get to the point where we would play only original symphony pieces and original symphonies, so the day they heard my favorite piece, *The New World Symphony* by Antonin Dvorak, then they would know that we had achieved our goal. The most important step would be motivating the adult players to believe that they could play at a higher level than they had ever thought they could do, and I would use Napoleon Hill's philosophy, "What the mind of man can conceive and believe, it can achieve." I was hired that day as the new conductor of the Huron Symphony, which was founded in 1956.

High School Music Contest

In the middle of March, I decided to enter my 9th graders in the state high school music competition, so I asked the high orchestra director if she had the form to register for the event. She stated that I could not enter my 9th graders because they were junior high and not high school. I tried to explain to her that high school activities start with 9th graders, and she disagreed, so I went to our local state music chairman, who was the owner of one of the music stores in Watertown. He said the same thing, that they could not enter the event because they were 9th graders. I knew that the rules for high school activities (sports & music) began in 9th grade, and it could go lower if you had an athlete with that kind of talent (for example, small-town golf), so I called the state's Activity Supervisor and told him of my dilemma.

The Supervisor agreed with me and sent me a form to register my group. He also said that he would call the regional chairperson and let him know his decision. This did not sit well with the music clique in Watertown. I had forty-five 9th graders, but my concertmaster was an 8th grader and I decided to let her lead the group. The contest was three weeks after my debut in Huron, and I was still flying high.

The day of the contest arrived, and I took 46 students out of class to make the 50-mile trip to Milbank, SD. As you can imagine, the junior high teachers were once again not happy. Before the music contest, I had my first junior high full orchestra concert the first week of April. We were entered as Watertown High School #2. My students, with our performance goals and playing in the public so many times, were upset with all the hurdles we had to make just to perform at this contest, so they wanted to beat the high school. The scores came out and Watertown #1 received a one-minus rating and Watertown #2 had a score of one-plus. The reason we scored higher was that we played one number that was the same, but we played it better than the high school.

It was an exceptionally good day, and we sang all the way back to junior high. There had been so many things happening that school year that I could not seem to catch my breath, and three weeks after the music contest, Martha gave me our third son, Matthew Philip Scales. When Matthew was born, he did not open his eyes and the doctor handed him to me. I looked down at Matthew and said, "Hello Matthew, this is Dad;" he opened his eyes and we just stared at each other, and I started to cry.

ORCHESTRA PERSONNEL-- +9TH GRADE   ~8TH GRADE   *7TH GRADE

1st Violin
+Erin Johnson
  Concert Mistress
~Brandy DeWall
~Jessica Witcher
*Wendy Determan
~Tracey Glessinger
~Nicole Berg
~Sonia Heiden
*Michelle Monteith
+Mika Neuberger
+Maria Jepsen
~Jodi Johnson
*Jana Taken
~Anna McAtee
*Robin Anderson
~Lori Struckman
~Jodee Lugert
*Jennifer Redlin
*Angie Coyne
~Laura Kannas
+Jay Hofer
*Brady Black
~Gary Moes
*Jessie Chapin
*Anne Beebe
*Michele Stroup

2nd Violin
+Patty Rieffenberger
  principal
+Pam Witt
+Angie Halling
~Rebekah Dean
~Tamara Harding
~Matt Stupnik
~Page Petrich
*Kari Lieffort
*Holly Lundgaard
*James Wittrock
~Nathan Gurgel
~Danelle Walsh
*Micah Gurgel
*Travis Rudebusch
~Janis Nerison
~Mike Brennen
*Kim Rieffenberger
+Kris Bue
*Pat Whitlock

+Peggy Knox
*Bobbi Jo Anderson
~Christina Iverson
*Angela Ehlebracht
~Jamie Cordell
~Jay Koehn
~Jimmy Hagen
~Mike Woertink
*Erin Stowell
*Holly Seuer
*Holly Zwieg
*Jessica Van Liere

Viola
+Melissa Moses-principal
+Nikki Wilkenr
~Laura Ford
+Nicholle Stahl
+Charity Larson
~Kristi Corey
~LaShawn Kannas
*Kendra Brinkman
~Melissa Decker
*Darcy Beck
~Charity Hendricks
*Justin Kauffman
*Melanie Eide
*Andy Glynn
~Shawna McBrien
*Brent Stricherz
*Kirby Boucher
*Martin Kroschel

Cello
+Anne Marie McFarland
  principal
+Kari Lindner
+Sarah Kannas
~JoAnn Falk
~Jill Haan
~Kris Reyerson
~Sarah Kirchmeier
*Carolyn Bue
*Amber Mack
*Becky Hemiller
*Jeremy German

Bass
~Andy Brandley
  Principal
~Joel Brunick
+Martha Feller
+Tom Engebretson
*Clint Larson
*Kevin Harrington
*Ross Kranz

Flute
Tracie Miller
Angie Nogelmeier
Leslie Mack
Maggie Rick
Bonnie Carter

Clarinet
Julie McFarland
Linda Fogelberg
Amy DeVille
Kara Negaard
Tera Brinkman

Oboe
Nicole LaFramboise
Amy Bogen

French Horn
Siri Hanson
Heather Herzog
Kiersten Thompson
Angie Kranz

Trumpet
Rob Lubbers
Lori Horstmeyer

Trombone
Cody Zwieg
Nathan Dean

Percussion
Adam Fox
Scott Marquardt

Summer 1990

It was now my fourth summer orchestra, and student numbers continued to grow. I had a lot of beginning players that summer, so many that it gave me another group level when grade school started in September. I saw the summer beginners three times a week for an hour for five weeks, so I could not put them in the same class as the beginners in the fall. I could then take any students from the last year and put them at the beginning of summer class if they were falling behind. This system had been working very well.

That summer I had a mother and her daughter come up to me and asked if she could play the violin. I said why not, and her mom said because her daughter did not have a thumb on her left hand. Her little girl's dream was to play violin and I told her that I would help her with her dream. This was not new to me, because when I was teaching in Hutchinson, I had a student come up to me after a recruiting class and say that she wanted to play the cello. The kid behind her stated that there was no way she could play the cello and when I asked why, the little girl raised her left hand and there was no thumb. I looked at her and said, "We are going to have a lot of fun on the cello."

As I was leaving the school, I stopped at the little girl's classroom and talked to her. I told her that because she did not have a thumb on her left hand that she would have to strengthen her fingers on her left hand. So, I gave her a hard tennis ball and told her to keep this and squeeze it in her left hand as much as possible and I would give her other exercises in the future. She asked if that meant she got a cello, and I told her I'd see her next week in class. This young lady played cello all through high school. She played for me when I took the Hutchinson High School to the Southwest Music Festival in Oklahoma City, where we received a one+ rating. The little girl from Watertown also played violin through high school.

One day after summer rehearsal the principal came up to me and said that Huron high school had just lost their orchestra director, and they were shutting the string program down for a year because they did not have time to hire another teacher at this short notice. This was terrible news; if the Huron string program stopped for a year, then they would lose about half of the program by missing a year of recruiting new students. This would hurt the Huron Symphony down the road, so to help I wrote a music curriculum where a music teacher could meet the string students on Saturday mornings and run the whole string program from 7:30 in the morning to 5:00 Saturday evening and even have a beginning string class. I sent the curriculum to the Superintendent of Huron Public Schools. The Superintendent of Huron Public Schools called me and asked if I would run that program, and what could I say. So, for the next year every Monday evening I drove to Huron for the symphony rehearsals, and every Saturday I drove to Huron to teach their string program. During this time, we had a newborn, and Martha was not a happy camper.

The summer string program had just finished up and I was looking forward to a lot of golf, but then the phone rang. On the other end of the line was the State Fair president. After introductions, she asked if I would be interested in directing a concert for Bob Hope.

I paused, then asked, "The real Bob Hope?"

She said, "Yes, would you like to do the show?"

It would require three rehearsals with the orchestra and a two-hour dress rehearsal with Mr. Hope and his wife Dolores Reade. I told her that I would be honored to do it. The only thing was that I had to give her my conducting fee for the Bob Hope Show. What do you charge Bob Hope? I told Martha that I would do it for $4,000, but I would say $6,000 to give myself a little wiggle room. I called the President back and said that I would do it for $6,000 and she immediately said, "Great!" and hung up. I felt like I was just beaten by a used car salesman.

Bob Hope Show

Three weeks before the Hope show, I got a package in the mail, and it was the music for the show. There was also a letter that said that Mr. Hope's music manager would give me a call to go over the tempos for each piece. I received his call that night, and he was a charming person. We spent nearly two hours on the phone going over music tempos and other musical effects that Mr. Hope preferred. He said Mr. Hope would be fine at the dress rehearsal, but good luck with Dolores, and he was right.

The rehearsals with the orchestra went well, and we were excited about the dress rehearsal. On the day of the rehearsal, Mr. Hope slowly walked into the rehearsal room. His music manager introduced him to me, and I introduced Mr. Hope to the orchestra. Mr. Hope thought that my name (Mr. Scales) was very cool. Mr. Hope sat about two feet from me on a high stool. As we moved through the pieces, checking tempos and dynamics, I would ask Mr. Hope if he felt comfortable with the articulation of his music. He would always say in a whisper, fine, Mr. Scales, the orchestra is doing a great job. I thought to myself, how will he do a 2-hour show, because we are not getting any energy from him at this dress rehearsal?

We finished the rehearsal with Mr. Hope, and Dolores walked in primed for bear. After a testy 30-minute rehearsal with Dolores, I realized that the only thing I liked about this person was her name because my mom's name was Dolores. It was now time for the performance, the orchestra was sitting on stage, and I did the last things that I needed to do to get ready to walk on stage, when it hit me that I would be conducting for Bob Hope in front of 10,000 people. I started to get nervous, but I hit that right pocket, said, "Do it Now," and before I knew it, I was in front of the orchestra. We finished playing Bob Hope's opening theme, *Thanks for the Memories*, and he walked out on stage. The crowd went wild.

Mr. Hope put his hand up to his eyes and said, "turn up the lights. I would like to see whom I'm singing to." They turned up the lights, and it was like someone plugged Bob in because he was bouncing around that stage like he was 40 years old again. The tempos we worked on in rehearsal were twice as fast, and the dynamics were crisp and snappy. After the show, I went backstage to see Mr. Hope. He was sitting in a chair dripping with sweat and once again looked his age. I asked Mr. Hope if I could have his autograph, and he gave it to me and said, "Mr. Scales, you did a fine job."

I walked back to my car and ran into a couple of orchestra members. One of the players said, "You know Phil, usually in rehearsals, you do a lot of smiling and putting everyone at ease, but you were a little different during the Hope rehearsals."

I told him that the Hope show was different because I knew that Bob would write his memoirs, and when someone asked him who was the worst conductor that he ever worked with, I did not want my name in that slot.

I drove the 100 miles back to Watertown with Martha, who played in the orchestra, but I was sad because I could not share this moment with my family in Pittsburgh. In 1990 there was no internet or cell phones, nothing but snail mail. I also thought it would be great if the boys back in Glenwood could see me conducting for Bob Hope.

Fall of 1990

The school year started with great news. I had a letter in my mailbox from the Chicago National Music Conference. They thanked me for sending the tape of my group and for getting the paperwork done so quickly. They also congratulated me for my group being selected to perform at the 1991 National Music Convention. This was great news because I had achieved my prediction of going there in five years. I went to the principal's office and shared the exciting news with him. He thought it was great but told me not to tell the students until he talked to the Superintendent. Later that afternoon, the principal came into my office to inform me that the Superintendent said that junior high students cannot take out-of-state trips during the school year.

I felt that it was just a play on words. The history teacher who had his students wear black garbage bags would take over 100 students to Washington D.C. with eight to ten chaperones (whose fee was paid by the students) right after school was out every year. So, this was okay, but the orchestra-earned trip was not. I tried not to look too upset because I had learned that I just got labeled the Angry Black Man every time I did that, so I did my best not to go there. It became a tough job never telling the students about this decision because their hard work put us there, but I kept it from the students for about two years.

I called the Superintendent of Huron Public Schools because I needed to set up times to visit the elementary fifth-grade classrooms to recruit new string players. He told me to just call the principals and set up a time to visit. I called the four elementary principals, and they said to contact the classroom teachers, which I did. The classroom schedule was all set, so I took a personal leave from Watertown to go to Huron to do my recruiting. I went straight to the classroom in Huron with four instruments tucked under my arms. EVERYTHING STOPPED when I walked into the school; even the teacher seemed a little startled. She said, "Are you Mr. Scales?"

And I assured her that I was. When I started the recruiting session, the teacher left and came back with the principal, and they both sat in the back of the room and watched me do my recruiting. It was a perfect session, and the kids were having a great time. After the session, I told the students that we would start classes in the high school orchestra room that Saturday morning.

The principal walked with me down the hall and said the strangest thing to me. She said, "You do not sound black on the phone."

I had the same experience at one of the other schools too. My teaching started that Saturday morning with the middle school students because their classes started at 7:30 a.m. during the week. The mid-morning courses were set up for the grade school string players, followed by the 55 beginners. I saved the high school for last, so they could sleep in, and their attitude was much better at this time on a Saturday. I explained to the high school students that I would like to involve some of them in the Huron Symphony, which took them by surprise. This was a good group, although small, but we could change that. It was a long year driving to Huron on Saturdays and Mondays. Still, it kept the program alive until they got another teacher. They hired Hans Petersen from Minnesota the following summer, and we became good friends.

I had another great recruiting year in Watertown. I sent seven 9th graders to the All-State Orchestra, the most ever. The Watertown string program sent a total of 21 students to All-State Orchestra, which was a record. The teachers from the west side of the state were starting to take notice of the number of students making All-State from Watertown. Once again, the teachers at the junior high were upset because these seven students would miss three days of school to go to All-State. While the students were in rehearsal at All-State, the music teachers attended the American String Teachers Association (ASTA) meetings.

I enjoyed these meetings because not everyone was a teacher but might have music studios and work outside public schools. Most of them had private students in the orchestra. I got to know many of them, and some would later start playing in the Huron Symphony for me. I hung out with a small group, Tish, Dan Witte (Aberdeen high school orchestra director), and Hans Petersen, the new teacher in Huron. In my first concert with the Huron Symphony, I had 47 players, with just 21 string players. After I became the official conductor of the Huron Symphony, I had 73 people on stage with 42 string players in the first concert. My October and December concerts were a big success, with the attendance going from 250 people to over 600 in the audience. The end of 1990 was ending, and it had been an excellent year for me; my family and I had just found out that Martha was due in June with our baby girl. So, what could 1991 bring us?

Children's Choir Director

I started the year by accepting two new positions in our church, one as the grade school choir director and the other as the high school choir director. One of the reasons they asked me was because of the way I handled students of all ages. I had kids from all economic and social backgrounds in my classes, and they knew that Mr. Scales treated all students with dignity and respect regardless of who they were or where they came from. I started a grade school honors orchestra, and we rehearsed after school on Wednesdays, which was a big plus for the program. The junior high school was big into doing cultural units; the history class would tell the history, and the cooking class would do the meals, and the sewing class would make the appropriate outfits. I suggested to them that we could put all of that together with music. We could put on a fashion show with food served before the event and we could even play soft music under the history part. The orchestra did a fantastic job with the music, and it provided an excellent experience for all.

I also did a musical unit with my orchestra every year. The students would watch a musical in class, like My Fair Lady, The Sound of Music, Fiddler on the Roof, Hello Dolly, On Golden Pond, The Wiz, Seven Bridges for Seven Brothers, Westside Story, and Mary Poppins. We would then play the music and take an exam on the movie. After watching the Wiz (the black version of The Wizard of Oz), one of the exam questions was, what character did you connect with? Matt, a six-foot-four basketball player, and violin player said he identified with Toto because all through the movie, Toto would run off to be by himself. He felt that is what he did all the time because he did not feel comfortable around many people. The previous year (when he was in 7th grade), Matt came to me and wanted to quit orchestra because the basketball coach told him that he could not do both. I took Matt into my office and pulled out my high school yearbook, and showed him a picture of my best friend, Charles Peterson. Charles was 6'9", and when he was in 7th grade, he was 6'4" and played the violin. The picture of Charles dunking the basketball was one of the pictures that I showed Matt. Also, I explained that I went to college on a sports (baseball & football) scholarship. Matt stayed in the orchestra and was a dominant force for Watertown's basketball team all through high school.

The School District changed teaching models on a frequent basis. We were currently using the Madeline Hunter discipline model but were shifting to a new discipline model called the Boys Town Model. I had used the same Madeline Hunter model in Hutchinson when I first started teaching. Her Model was classified as a standard behavioral technique of direct instruction and modified operant conditioning. I liked the Boys Town Model so much that I became one of the instructors for teaching it to the district. The Boys Town behavioral model fit right in with my style of teaching my orchestra students. It called for the teacher to look that student in the eye and have them repeat the behavioral act and demonstrate the proper way to do it. This was easy for my students because I did individual playing in front of the whole class, so doing the Boys Town behavioral demonstration was easy for my classes.

This was my last semester to finish my Master of Education with a minor in conducting. Professor John F. Colson was my advanced conducting teacher. The junior high principal, Mr. Albertson, was my mentor for the last semester of my master's degree. I worked with him to set the entire school schedule for the next year, and I could now see the problem the orchestra was causing because of its large numbers.

We still did not have a room. I also did the noon supervising of all the lunches because that is what the principal did, and I enjoyed doing that part of the job. I had one project to finish that summer, and it was on classroom discipline. Then I would do my Oral and Writing exams in July and graduate in December. I had a fun year working with the Huron public school string program, and our year-end concert went very well. The program was in a good position, and the right hire could put the program on a growing track. I took my 9th graders to the State Music Contest in Milbank that April (no obstacles that year), and we received a 1+ on our performance.

The Hardest Summer of My Life

The summer orchestra program started with over 140 students enrolled from grade school to junior high. That year, they added band and vocal classes. On June 12th, our baby girl arrived, and on June 15th, I was on the road to Miami to pick up the girls. I now had 8 kids in the house, and my workload was a strain on me. First, I was adding a sunken living room, bathroom, and laundry room at home, and also adding a two-tier deck on the back of the addition. I was doing all the work, and my father-in-law, Mel, was the supervisor, since he had Parkinson's Disease. I still had summer orchestra in the morning, and then had to drive fifty miles to South Dakota State University twice a week for a two-hour class. I still had to turn in my classroom discipline plan, so I did my project on the Boys Town Model. One day after summer orchestra class, I got a group of orchestra students and five of my kids together. I put them in a classroom and taped how I worked with the Boys Town Model in the school. Once I got home, I would spend a couple of hours working on the new addition and then off to the park to spend some time with the kids. Once the little kids were down for the night, I would study until 2:00 a.m. because my writing exam was in a couple of weeks, and if I passed that, I would have my Orals two days after that. After about a week of this pace, I could see that Martha needed a break from my crazy pace. So, we decided that she and baby Caitlin would go down to her beloved Indiana for a family wedding and some much-needed rest with her Indiana family, who were all terrific people.

So, I continued to do what I needed to do, and Eunice and Mel were the best grandparents ever to all the kids. The day arrived for my

85

written exam, scheduled for eight hours. You walk into a room, and all you have is a pencil. Remember, this was before computers, and you could not use a typewriter. They gave you 10 questions about your field, and you had to answer eight. After five hours, I gave them 80 handwritten pages of answers. My writing finger was bleeding, and I had a massive headache. I felt that I had done well, but I had to wait for that phone call from SDSU, and it came that night. I had passed my Written exams, and my Orals were scheduled for two days later.

Martha was back home, so I could hit the studies hard. I stood outside the room, waiting for someone from my panel to come and get me. One of my professors opened the door and told me that it was time. So, I tapped that right pocket and said, "Do it Now."

There were six professors seated around the table. I had five for class, but I did not know one of the professors, and that is the way they wanted it. The professors started firing questions at me. I was scheduled for four hours, but after 2 ½ hours, they told me to step into the hall until they reached a decision. I walked to the end of the hall, got a drink of water, and felt like I would throw up (but I did not). When they called me back into the room, they told me that I was the first African American to get a Master of Education Degree from SDSU. That did not matter to me, but I was glad to be the first in my family to have a master's. I got back home and celebrated with my family. The girls were going back to Miami in a couple of days, and I would miss them, but the boys needed time to adjust to their little sister and our family unit.

One day before the girls were going home, my oldest daughter Tashai (14) was sitting on a chair, bawling her eyes out and we asked her what the problem was. She said she did not want to go back to Miami but wanted to live with us. I called my ex-wife and told her what Tash had said, and she accused me of putting her up to it. So, the first thing I did was put off the kids' return until I could get Tash in front of a judge, which we did, and the judge talked to Tash alone for two hours. When she came out, the judge told me the court would let her stay in Watertown, so I took the other girls back, and five years later, Tashai graduated from Watertown High School.

The summer was coming to an end, and I got a call from the Superintendent from Huron, and he told me they had hired Hans Petersen as the new orchestra teacher. I gave Hans a call to welcome him to South Dakota and talk about the students that would be in his program, and welcomed him to play in the symphony. He accepted the offer. Hans was a fine violinist and would be a great addition to the symphony.

The school year had begun, and we had some changes in junior high. The first change was I now had three classes at the junior high, and I also had a homeroom with 20 students reporting to me at the beginning of school. Being at the junior high meant that they had to hire another string teacher, to cover some of my string classes in the grade schools. The person they hired had also applied for the junior high position when I did, and we got along very well. She played for me in the Huron Symphony. I did not change the recruiting style because I did the recruiting, and she would teach the students that signed up. I had the sixth-grade honors orchestra in place, so I still got to see most of the students. The tradition of playing a string instrument under Mr. Scales was already underway.

I now felt more connected to junior high because of having three classes plus a homeroom. The students in my homeroom were not orchestra students, so I had the opportunity to meet different students. The word was out that Mr. Scales was not the teacher to try any bad behavior. I had one class in the vocal teacher's room and two in the band room, which did not sit well with the band teacher.

The junior high band director never got along with me. We went to the same church, and I had her daughter in the church choir. She had a beautiful voice and later became a professional opera singer with the Cincinnati Opera. The band teacher felt that the band room was exclusively hers, even if I was teaching a class. She would walk in and start writing her lesson plans on the board for her next class, right behind my back while I was teaching. Even the students thought that this was rude. One day I asked her if she had a problem with my race, and she said that she could not be prejudiced because she had sold her house to a Black man. This threw me for a loop because there were only two Black men in town, and why would she say that?

Having more time at the junior high gave me more time to help train the teachers on the Boys Town Model. The school year moved quickly, and all of a sudden it was December. I got home late one night from lessons at school, and Martha told me that I had a parent waiting in my new sunken living room. As I opened the door, I saw this lady with her back to me, and my first thought was, who is this Black lady sitting on my couch? The lady turned towards me, and it was my

Mom. I could have cried because she flew from Pittsburgh to attend my master's graduation, which was in two days. I proudly walked across the stage, and Mom noticed that I was the only Black person getting a master's degree. The day was certainly a day to remember because Mom was there, and so were my oldest daughter and the rest of the family. My Mom stayed until after Christmas, which made the holiday even more special.

Master's Ceremony - My mother, father-in-law, mother-in-law, sister-in-law, and my children Tashai, Michael, and Jason

Chapter Seven
The High Bar

I had so far done seven concerts with the Huron Symphony, and we had performed the *Gayane Ballet Suites, Scheherazade, The Hebrides Overture, Polovtsian Dances, Marche Slav, Overture to Zampa, Pictures at an Exhibition, Schubert's Unfinished Symphony,* and *Vivaldi's The Four Seasons.* I had told the orchestra members that I would raise the bar for them after each concert until we could play Dvorak's *New World Symphony.*

Our fall performance of Vivaldi's *Four Seasons* started off with a bit of drama. I headed out for the concert in Huron, which was 100 miles from Watertown, and in the van, I had Martha, Art, and two of my top students who were also members of the symphony. I was 20 miles outside Huron, and I had a tire blowout. I had to get everyone out of the car to change the tire. All the tire lugs came off except one, and I could not get it off. One of the symphony members came by, and I had him take all my riders with him and said I would be along as soon as I got the lug off. After they left, I ran to a farmer's house, and he came over with a welding torch and got the lug off. I got to the dress rehearsal at 4:45 and it was over at 5:00. I thanked everyone for waiting so patiently, and I thanked the South Dakota String Quartet for joining us at this concert. I told the Quartet that the symphony had worked extremely hard to perform the *Four Seasons*, and they knew the music well, and I knew that the Quartet had their parts down.

So, I said "Trust me tonight, and everything will be great. Have a good dinner, and I will see you at the Barn."

We did not play a single note before the concert.

I was about to walk on stage, but I took just a little longer because I needed to get my thoughts in order. I tapped my right pocket and said, "Do it Now."

I walked out on stage, and the orchestra gave an outstanding performance. I could feel the orchestra's trust in me, and I knew it was time to raise the bar. So, in 1992 it was time for *The New World*

Symphony, and the first thing the orchestra asked was what movement we were doing. I asked the group what was the one thing I always said before working on any music with them, and they said that I always asked them to trust me. So, I replied, I am asking you to trust me again because I am ready to teach you all four movements.

The ages in the symphony ranged between 14 to 84, so the younger players needed to truly understand the music. And that is what I taught as the group learned to play the music. It was an incredible journey watching and hearing the orchestra dive into this work. I worked with this group once a week for two hours, and the concert was two months away. I was confident that we could do this piece, but I also knew that I would be pushing two sections extremely hard, the celli and the horn sections. The horn players were good, but they would have to raise their playing level because the New World was 45 minutes of solid playing, and the lips could falter.

The day of the concert arrived, and we were at the dress rehearsal; everything went well, we stopped a couple of times to tighten things up, but overall, it was solid. We all went to the Barn to have dinner, and the orchestra members looked a little nervous, which I had sensed in the rehearsal. The orchestra members took their seats, and I was ready to walk on stage. It dawned on me why the orchestra could be a little nervous, because we had never played *The New World Symphony* without stopping. So, I tapped my right pocket two times, said, "Do it Now."

And walked briskly onto the stage. I stood on my podium, looked at each section, and whispered, "Trust Me."

I put the baton up, and we were ready to begin. The piece starts with slow-moving passages, and I milked them to build confidence in the orchestra to let them know that we were doing this. We confidently moved through the movements. The first movement was outstanding, and the second movement was very moving to me, because Dvorak wrote it about the enslaved people in the south (from the negro spiritual *Going Home*). The third movement was based on Native American rhythms, and the fourth was the energy of the great frontier. In the fourth movement at the end, the horn's lips got a little tired, but it was only a couple of notes. I have always told my students that if they make a mistake, make the audience forget it by playing their best at the end, which is what the horns did that night. I was immensely proud of them because they would never have thought they could play at this level a year ago. You can hear our performance of the New World Symphony on my YouTube channel - Conductor Phil Scales. The video is not clear, but the music is genuine.

The March concert was now behind us, and I was turning forty in thirty days (April 7th). The junior high staff had a tradition where on your 40th birthday, they would announce it over the intercom. Later in the morning, they would have a birthday cake in the teacher's lounge in your honor, and some teachers would wear black armbands. During the morning announcement, I did not hear my name, but that was okay because I knew I would have a cake in the teachers' lounge mid-morning. I got back from the grade schools mid-morning and went into the teachers' lounge, and there it was - a beautiful cake. So, I cut the cake and passed out pieces, taking one to the principal and one to the secretary. I felt like I was finally being respected for my efforts in junior high, because I had been included in the birthday traditions.

I went home for lunch and told Martha about the cake, and she had tears in her eyes because she bought the cake. Martha had called the secretary to see if I had a cake there. When the secretary said no, Martha bought a cake and took it to junior high because she did not want me to be disappointed. I did not want to go back to school that afternoon.

I began working on our May concert, which seemed to fall on Mother's Day most of the time. I was coming back from a rehearsal on Monday night with Art and two of my top viola players. One of the girls reminded me of my promise to take them to the National Music Conference in Chicago. This was the first time I had ever mentioned anything about that trip, and I told the girls that we won the trip a couple of years ago, but the Superintendent would not allow junior high students to go out of state, so we could not accept the honor of playing at the conference. One of the girls said I should do it myself, then, and that was the seed that started the Watertown Youth Symphony.

The Beginning of a New Orchestra

The school year ended on another high, and I had my annual orchestra picnic at the zoo, where I would supply grilled hot dogs, chips, cookies, and all the soda they could drink. The parents would drop the kids off for two hours. I gave out the orchestra awards, but the most important award for orchestra I always saved for the all-school awards. This award was given to the person I thought was caring, respected, trustworthy, reliable, and would do what they said they would do. I started this award in my second year at junior high school, and I named it the Art Cirulis Award. If you won this award, you were a person of high character.

The summer program was all set up, and this year I added a group called the Watertown Youth Symphony. This group would be a full orchestra, so I would need support from the wind players in Watertown, but I did not get that support. I had 40 string players and only three wind players, a trumpet, flute, and clarinet. So, I had to rethink this project if I was going to run it in the fall.

One day during the summer, I ran into one of the wealthiest ladies in Watertown (and South Dakota.) Her name was Vera Way Marghab, and she owned Marghab Linens. She and her husband Emile founded Marghab Linens, Ltd., on the Portuguese island of Madeira in 1933. Together, Emile, a native of Cyprus (then a British Colony), and Vera Way, a native of Watertown, South Dakota, established one of the finest embroidery houses in Madeira. Marghab Linens flourished for forty-seven years (1933-1980), according to Wikipedia. The Marghab Collection at the South Dakota Art Museum was started in 1970 with the donation of nearly 800 pieces by Vera.

She was very fond of classical music and asked me if I thought it was time for Watertown to have a symphony. She had heard from a friend of hers in Huron that the Huron Symphony was great. I told her that I would get back to her and let her know. For the next several days, I went to all the music people in town to see how they felt about starting a symphony orchestra. I was disappointed by the results I received, although I probably shouldn't have been. It turned out that a few of the top musicians in Watertown did not want to start one if I was the conductor, because I was "just" a junior high teacher. This wasn't going to deter me, so I called Ms. Marghab and told her that I would begin the process of legally forming a Symphony Orchestra.

I wrote the bylaws for the group, got a lawyer to do all the legal paperwork, and we secured a non-profit number. I formed a symphony board and began selecting my players.

The high school orchestra director never played in the symphony, nor did a couple of top string teachers in the area. The grade school string instructor we had hired, however, graciously played every concert in Huron and Watertown. I had to keep a positive attitude about the Watertown Symphony because everyone said that it could not be done. If I did it, it would not be very "professional." They said I was just a junior high director and did not know music literature. None of these people had heard or seen me conduct the Huron Symphony. So, I started handpicking my personnel, selling memberships, selling newspaper ads, securing concert dates, securing the high school stage, securing a rehearsal site, and consistently securing donations.

The board president was Joanita Monteith, and her daughter was one of my top violin players. We worked very well together, and Joanita did the artwork for the program cover and ran all the board meetings. Before the first rehearsal, I had sold over 100 season tickets and had 61 musicians committed to playing for me. So, in the first week of September 1992, the Watertown Symphony had its first rehearsal.

I was still at a standstill on what I should do with the Youth Symphony because I was not getting any support from the Watertown High School wind players. I called my band friend (Tish) from Sisseton and asked if any of his players would be interested in playing in the Youth Symphony on Saturday mornings for three-hour rehearsals. After listening to me, Tish said, "What do you need?"

And I replied, "What can you send?"

I knew this would be a great fit because he ran his program the same way I did - respect earns respect. I then called small-town band directors in the area to see if they had any students looking to play in an orchestra. When I had my first rehearsal, we had 3 flutes, two clarinets, 2 trombones, 3 trumpets, 2 horns, 3 percussion players, one oboe, and 45 string players. We also picked up a few string players that lived outside of Watertown. It was disappointing that there was only one wind player from Watertown, and he was my 1st trumpet player. This young man played for three years for me.

I ran the Youth Symphony all on my own because not one business would support the new Youth Symphony, even though over the years we took eight out-of-state trips in a row. So, with the fall school year up and running, I added two more days to my workload. Monday nights, I had the Huron Symphony, and on Tuesday nights, I conducted the Watertown Symphony. On Wednesday nights, I taught four hours at Mt. Marty College. On Thursday nights, I gave music lessons until 7:30, Friday night was reserved for football games at the stadium with Michael & Jason to watch the Arrows play, and Saturday morning was Youth Symphony. Sunday was always up in the air because I played viola in the SDSU Symphony under John Colson and in Northern University's Symphony under Joe Koob.

My concerts were on Saturday nights in Huron and Sunday afternoons in Watertown. All of this was done while teaching all day. The school year also brought something new to the Scales family, a new member. It was the first week of October, and I got a call from my ex-wife Carell and her husband Paul. She had remarried years ago and had another girl and a boy. She and Paul called me because they could not handle Nadia's behavior and asked if I would take her for a year because she was totally out of control. I agreed, and now my oldest two daughters were the only Black students at the Watertown Jr. High. (Tashai was now in 8th grade and Nadia would be in 7th grade) Nadia was a little much for the staff at Watertown. It took me a few months to see a difference in her attitude, but it did come, and she had become a delightful young lady to be around. She started to enjoy what our family life was all about on an everyday basis. I now had six of my kids living with me, and my wife deserved the wife of the year award.

The Watertown Youth Symphony

The best way to tell the Watertown Youth Symphony story is by telling the whole story at once. The Youth Symphony was formed because of a promise. I had promised my first recruiting class that I would take them to Chicago to play at the National Music Convention one day. They earned the trip, but the Superintendent said that junior high students could not go out of state, even though an eighth-grade teacher took students to D.C. every summer. So, I wanted our South Dakota students to see a little bit of the world, so the Youth Symphony would need to be an independent traveling group.

We would have four concerts during the school year and travel in the summer. I could not get any sponsors in the community to support the Youth Symphony, but that just meant that it was my baby. At our first rehearsal, I told the kids that our first trip would be to San Antonio, Texas, for ten days during the first week of June. The first rehearsal went better than I had hoped. I thought it would take a while for all the students to adjust to my conducting and teaching style, but it did not. I knew that the Watertown kids would be on the ictus of the beat, but so were the Sisseton kids. When I stopped, you could hear a pin drop. I knew that Tish and I handled our students the same way, but to see it working so well was fantastic. We held rehearsals in the junior high and the concerts in the junior high gym or at the park & rec gym/auditorium. We usually had about 200-250 people at our concerts, but I never had any administrators or teachers come to the concerts, except for one teacher who came because her daughter was a member of the group.

San Antonio, Texas

While planning the concerts throughout the year I also had to plan our first trip. The students would have to participate in all the fundraisers, and I would record each student's account. As a member of the Youth Symphony, you could not avoid the fundraisers because a parent could not just write a check for his or her child. As a member, the students had to do their best to raise their own money, and if they then fell short, parents could help. I firmly believed that if a parent just wrote a check for the trip, then the student had no ownership of it and would not enjoy it as much as the students who had worked their tails off to go. Any parent who wanted to be a chaperone also had rules to follow. I would have a chaperone for every four students, and they would be responsible for those kids, but you could not be a chaperone for your child's group. I reasoned that some kids could control their parents, so they could then control the group.

Everyone also had to sign an agreement that I was the only person in charge because if there was a problem, everyone would know who would handle it, and it would just make things go more smoothly. I also made the room assignments. In rehearsals, the kids hung out with the students they knew from their school, but I wanted them to form a long-term relationship with the students from other towns as well. When we were on a trip, we were the Watertown Area Youth Symphony from South Dakota, and making sure students got to really know each other on the trips via room assignments worked well.

We had a variety of fundraisers, such as selling steaks, fruit, magazines, and play-a-thons (we did a 24-hour play-a-thon at Hy-vee at Christmas time). We also did a Snowman-A-Thon, where one Saturday morning we went out and made 300 snowmen in front of the junior high. This first trip allowed me to somewhat keep my promise to my first recruiting class. Instead of Chicago, though, we were soon headed on chartered buses to San Antonio. My first class of students were now juniors in high school and were excited about heading to Texas. This was the only trip that Martha did not make because we had five kids at home and our daughter was quite young at the time.

The students loved the drive to San Antonio, and some of the students had never been out of South Dakota before. We had a few playing engagements sprinkled around some fun activities, including Sea World, San Antonio Zoo, Six Flags Over Texas, and the Alamo. One of our performances was at the Riverwalk, and it was an outdoor event. The Riverwalk is a city park and network of walkways along the banks of the San Antonio River, one story beneath the streets of San Antonio. The river runs in front of the stores, and there is a performance place outside. This is where we had our first concert in Texas, but it was a little windy, so I told the students to grab a few clothespins to hold their music. One of my students, Andy B. (R.I.P.), was a bass player from my first class, and he grabbed a large handful of clothespins and had them clipped around his tall wire stand. Andy must have had 20 clothespins around his stand and laughed at the kids whose music was blowing off their stand. Then suddenly, I could feel a strong wind on my back, and I looked at Andy just in time to see the wind pick his whole wire stand up and dump it in the river. No one else could see this because Andy was behind them.

Andy looked at me and then the river, and we both watched his stand sink like a rock. Andy then *Improvised, Adapted, and Overcame* his problem by quickly moving to the next bass player's stand. Still, I have never forgotten his face when his stand sank.

Setting up on the River Walk

Kristi Corey, Lynnette Mack, Melissa Decker, and Brandi DeWall at the San Antonio Zoo

When we got back home, I had a banquet for the students and parents, and the students ran the program. They told great stories about each other, and you could tell that many friendships developed during the trip, which is what I wanted. The most important thing I learned is that we could make these trips. So, when it was my turn on the program, I announced where we were going the next year.

The next trip involved driving to Miami, then boarding the SS Britannis as the featured music group, and sailing to Nassau, Bahamas, to perform at the Market Square. Summer of '94, we headed to Miami in a vast, chartered bus (60 passengers) plus a 15-passenger van pulling an equipment trailer. The trip took take 40 hours with no long stops. The students were fired up getting on the bus, but that faded about 12 hours into the trip. We stopped in Orlando, stayed at the fancy Atlantis Hotel, and had pizza poolside, which helped the kids forget about the long drive we had just made.

The following day, we drove the final four hours to Miami, boarded the SS Britannis, and cruised to Nassau, Bahamas. This was a dream come true for many students, and I enjoyed watching them roam the ship. My daughter made this trip as an oboist. We were scheduled to perform at the Market Square the next day, and we rehearsed that evening on the ship. When we got to the Square, there were no chairs for the group, and the organizer said he thought it was a band playing. So, I ran around trying to find chairs for the cello players because they could not stand and play. I found enough chairs, but that was not the only problem, and we all discovered at once that it was the heat. The temperature was 96 with no shade, and the first player to drop was Heidi H., a violin player. Then students began dropping like flies. The chaperones were running water out to the kids, and I decided to cut the program short. So, we packed up and let the students cool off and enjoy the rest of the day.

Nassau, Bahamas - Market Square

That night we were the featured group, and we had dinner with the cruise captain. I was so proud of the kids because they were dressed up for the occasion and represented South Dakota well. The ship started to roll a little by the end of dinner, when we were set to play. While we were on the Island, one of the percussion players bought a small steel drum and wanted to know if he could play it on the number *Jammin' in Jamaica* that we would perform. I told him he had three hours to make it work, and being one of Tish's kids, I knew it would happen. As we started to play, the ship rocked even more, and I could see some of the students turning a bit green. My first clarinet player (a friend of my daughter) then threw up into her clarinet, and it came out all the holes in her clarinet.

It was a scene that I wish I had not witnessed. The clarinet player looked up at me, and I nodded toward the restroom, and she got up and left the stage. No one else lost it that night, but we will never forget that sight. The audience received the last number *Jammin' in Jamaica* well, and Curtis nailed the steel drum part. The cruise ended, and we were back on the bus heading back to South Dakota. The bus broke down in Tennessee, and we had a two-hour delay, but the students were great about the delay. We then had to stop at a motel to pick up the new driver, and when he did not answer his door, the students waited in a store and watched Nicole Brown Simpson's murder investigation on TV. The new driver finally showed up, and we made it safely back to South Dakota. The trip went great, but the one thing I decided is that we would never drive that far again. So, on the next trip, we would drive only as far as Minneapolis (4 hours), then board a plane, and fly to Stockholm, Sweden, for 12 days.

Phil, Martha, and chaperones

Stockholm, Sweden

How does one decide to take a group of students overseas to a place that traveling groups usually don't visit? I had a parent who was a teacher's aide at one of the grade schools, and I had two of her kids in the orchestra. Nora was from Stockholm, and she dropped the idea of a student exchange program between the Youth Symphony and a high school in Stockholm. Nora gave me the name of her high school teacher Erik Hermansson, who was also a composer. He was open to the idea but said he had not planned a trip for his students, but we could now start planning with my group. So, my students would come over to Stockholm and stay with the local students, which meant the cost of the trip would be less expensive for the students.

Meeting our host families

When we arrived in Stockholm with 60 students & 20 chaperones, we went to the high school for dinner and a concert. After the concert, we had the students meet their host families, and I gave the kids the time that we would meet in the morning. Martha and I went to Mr. Hermansson's home, and we talked for a couple of hours, and then Mr. Hermansson took us upstairs to our bedroom. As we reached the top of the steps, there was a bedroom, and Erik said that this would be my bedroom and then took Martha down the hall to her room. I did not know what to say, but this was his house and his rules. Later that night, I left my room to go to Martha's. The wood floors were very creaky, but I made it without waking anyone up.

A little while later, the sun hit me in my face, and I jumped out of bed, thinking that I had overslept, but it was the midnight sun and only 2:00 a.m. I went back to sleep thinking that I could play golf at 2:00 am in Sweden. In the morning, Erik explained that he put me in a different room because he thought Americans did not sleep together in single beds, which is all he had in his home. I asked Erik what piece he had been playing on his piano the previous evening, and he said that it was something that he had been working on. He explained during summers in the "land of the midnight sun" people went to bed very late, so he usually played and composed until very late at night.

The students had their first performance at the Grand Hotel Saltsjöbaden, one of Stockholm's finest hotels. I kept the students out late because I did not want them to be a burden on their host families. But after a couple of days, the host families asked if they could have more time with our kids, so I changed our schedule to meet their request. The students saw many exciting things, such as the Vasa Museum, where they could walk aboard a 17th-century ship that sank in the harbor on its maiden voyage. They also saw the Royal Palace, and we spent time at the Gröna Lund theme park. We also spent a lot of time in the Gamla Stan - the Old Town of Stockholm. The last night I took the kids on a cruise just for us, and we stopped on an island where the crew lit bonfires and a live band had us dancing the night away.

Performance at the Grand Hotel Saltsjöbaden

The trip was a success, and before we left, we made a final stop at the Hard Rock Café in Stockholm.

That night Mr. Hermansson gave me the piece that he had been composing, a Concerto for Viola and Orchestra. He knew that I was a viola player, and he wrote it for me. I was so touched, and I would later premier this Concerto with the Watertown Symphony. The next day, we walked into the airport with Tish leading from the front and me following up in the rear. As I got closer to the head of the line, I could hear a buzz of voices, signaling a problem. The problem was that the Swedish airlines had gone on strike and to make room, they had split my group up; half would leave today, and the other group would fly out tomorrow. As you can imagine, students were excitedly offering to stay behind in Sweden an extra day.

I went to the front of the line and explained to the clerk that we had to be in Chicago today, and I had no way of contacting parents to let them know that half the students would not be home today (this was pre-cell phones.) She said she could not help me, so I asked her to speak to her supervisor. I explained the situation to the supervisor, and he said the same thing. So, I calmly asked to see his supervisor and finally got the answer I had to have, that we could board the plane, which was fifteen minutes before takeoff. Once we got to Chicago, I told all the students and chaperones to check at the counter and ensure they had a seat on the plane to Minneapolis because of the mess in Stockholm. Everyone had a seat on the plane except me, and I told them that if I did not fly, everyone with the Watertown Symphony did not fly.

The boarding began, and everyone from my group was on the plane except me. I went to the counter and asked if I would get a seat, and the lady said that she did not think I would get on the plane. So, I asked her to make an announcement to my group, and she said she could do that, so I told her to tell all Watertown people to get off the plane because they would not fly without me. She called her supervisor, and he came over, hit a few buttons, gave me a ticket, and told me to have a great flight. I did not have to go far on the plane because I was sitting in first class.

After we returned home, I was at our local hardware store and was chatting with the clerk about the trip. One of the retired music teachers in Watertown was standing next to me at the other check-out lane. She said that I should be ashamed of myself for wearing "that awful shirt" and that I should not be around kids. I was thrown for a loop because I could not remember what I had on at that moment, so I glanced at my shirt.

It said: The Hard Rock Café in Stockholm, so I looked at the clerk and asked her if she knew anything about this place, and she said, "Well, isn't it a hamburger place?"

And the retired teacher stormed out of the store. We looked at each other, and the clerks said in amazement, "What is her problem?"

The night of the banquet was a success, and for the first time, I could really see the students come together as the Watertown Youth Symphony. So, it was time for me to put this group in a competition situation so we could see where we ranked. I asked the students if they believed in magic because next summer, we were headed to Disney World for a competition, a cruise, and a layover on the island of Freeport, Bahamas.

Our First Competition - Disney World

The orchestra was focused all year, and the students came to Saturday rehearsals with a lot of energy. One unforgettable Saturday, though, one of my string players told me that her cousin, who was also in the group, had committed suicide the night before. I told the students they could leave if they wanted because I would not hold a rehearsal, but I would stay at the school if the kids wanted to be with each other. All the kids spent the whole rehearsal comforting each other, and you could see the bond between these kids. I was so glad that I had pushed with this group because they were an extraordinary group of kids.

I thought our Disney trip would be easier, because we had chartered buses taking us to Sioux Falls airport (only 100 miles away). Then we would fly to Orlando and take a bus to the hotel. The bus trip was short and quick, but a storm popped up, and we had a delay in Sioux Falls, which made our connection to St. Louis very tight. I had 60 people with me, and an additional 15 people were scheduled to be on that St. Louis connection to Orlando as well. When we got to St. Louis, they told us that we had missed the flight and that they could get us out the following day. So, my group and the other 15 people were just stranded. The other 15 passengers started to leave, but I asked them to wait a few minutes until I talked to someone. I went to the ticket counter and asked the lady why a plane would take off when they knew that 75 people were already in the air trying to get there. She said that she did not have an answer, so I asked to see someone who could give me that answer. I finally got someone else, and I told him that the students had worked hard all year to raise money to make this competitive trip. They needed to be in Orlando today by 6:00 pm. I asked again if someone could tell me why the plane left without 75 people. I never got upset, but I was steadfast.

Finally, I got a call from a different supervisor who asked me to give him a few minutes to see what he could do. He said he understood my position and my responsibility to so many people. About ten minutes later, I was called to the front desk for a phone call. The person at the other end first said that he was sorry that we had to go through this and that he had taken care of the problem. My group would be flying to Miami on two charter airplanes that would hold 40 people on each plane. Once we got to Miami, my group would board another large plane to take us to Orlando. He said that the only problem was we wouldn't get into Orlando until 4:00, but that was not a problem because we did not play until 9:00 am the following day.

I told the students (and the other very grateful 15 people) that we boarded in 15 minutes. Someone from the other group asked one of my students who I was, and she said, "We call him Mr. Scales."

The flight to Miami went smoothly, as did the connection to Orlando. We arrived at the hotel at 5:30, and the poolside pizza party was at 6:30 and lights out at 11:00. The following day everyone showed up for breakfast with their performing shirts on. Our performing shirts were Smurf blue, with magenta/purple letters. The front had The Watertown Youth Symphony written on it, and the back had the faces of Mount Rushmore (the pride of South Dakota) with the lettering "Great Faces Great Places." I designed these shirts because they looked great when everyone was together, and they showcased where the group was from. Plus, you could see these shirts a mile away, which was great when all the kids were turned loose in Disney World.

The performance was at Disney World in one of the open-air shelter auditoriums. There were over twenty groups, and each group performed in front of three judges. The Youth Symphony was on stage, and I took a little time to get my thoughts together before taking the stage. I thought about where this group started and where we were now. The kids on stage now were the brothers and sisters of the first class of students that I started. My current concertmistress, Katie, was the younger sister of my first concertmistress in the summer of '87. I took the stage, looked down at the orchestra, and lifted my baton. Their playing was strong, energetic, and very musical. After everyone played, they spent the rest of the day in the park. The awards would be given out later at the same outdoor auditorium.

The students were on their own at the park, so Martha, Tish, Cindy (his girlfriend), and I were on our own as well. As we walked through the park, we would spot our Smurf blue shirts everywhere. We were in Epcot Center and stopped in Morocco and saw about eight of our girls, all from different schools, dancing up a storm. Later that afternoon, everyone reported back to the shelter for the award ceremony. The Youth Symphony members were sitting in the back, and we could see all the trophies lined up on the stage and my students were wondering if they would get one of the big ones. They called out the first-place groups last, but we could see and feel the excitement from the other groups as they ran up to the stage to get the award when their school was called. They started calling first-place winners, and the announcer said, "Will the Watertown Youth Symphony please come down."

The group went wild, and they turned to me, and I told them to go and get their trophy. I saw five students running to the stage to pick up the first-place award. We had just achieved something special without the support of most of the people in Watertown, but we did it anyway, and seeing the excited smiles on my students' faces made me feel proud.

Youth Symphony wins first contest

A week ago today, 41 members of the Watertown Area Youth Symphony "came unglued" in Orlando, Fla. They had just been told that their four year-old orchestra placed first in the open division of the Orlando Music Fest.

"The open division would be double A's down there, like the size of Watertown High School," explained the orchestra conductor Phil Scales.

Watertown's symphony competed against about 250 other youth music groups in the fest, which was open to bands and orchestras. Most of the competitors were bands. The groups competed over a 12-week period which ended last Saturday with the announcement of the winners.

"The kids just came unglued when they announced it," Scales said.

The Music Fest was the first competition for the Watertown orchestra, which was already in Florida for some performances plus a trip to Freeport, Bahamas.

"We were at the point that we needed to enter a competition," Scales said.

He chose this one after hearing about it on a previous youth orchestra summer trip three years ago.

The music groups each performed two pieces on a specified weekend of the competition. They received both individual and overall ratings. To advance to the second, overall competition, a group had to receive either a superior or an excellent. Watertown was rated excellent.

Scales said he had no great expectations for the orchestra's first contest. "I was kind of like Rocky, I just didn't want to get an honorable mention!" he jokes.

The Watertown Area Youth Symphony performed "Rhosymedre" by Vaughan Williams and the "Slavonic Dances" by Dvorak.

Following the competition, the orchestra spent a day touring MGM studios, then took a three-day trip to the Bahamas, where they also performed. They returned to Watertown on Thursday.

For the summer, the orchestra will be primarily a string group. In the fall, the group's regular schedule of four concerts will be resumed. Next summer, the group plans a trip to London.

FIRST PLACE — Youth symphony conductor Phil Scales stands with the first-place trophy his orchestra won at last week's Orlando Music Fest. (Public Opinion photo by Carol Andring)

We had two more days in Disney World, and the students asked me if they could wear something other than the Smurf blue shirts because they were getting a little potent with the smell. So, I told everyone to wash their shirt out that night and they could wear something different the next day. The next day at Disney, I did not see a single student for five hours, and that worried me. The next day we were back to Smurf blue, and I could spot the kids just fine.

After four days in Miami, we boarded the Carnival Fantasy Cruise and went to Freeport, Bahamas, where we stayed on the island for two days. The first night our tour guide from Straight-A-Tours took Martha and me to a restaurant named Pier One. This was a restaurant where they had a glass floor, and you could see sharks swimming under your feet. I was nervous the whole time. The female chaperones gave me a day off on the second day, so Tish, Trevor (a former student and now a chaperone), and I went golfing. It was fun until the sky opened and dropped a ton of rain on us, so much that we had water sloshing around in the golf cart. I started thinking of crocodiles, alligators, snakes, and iguanas, so we quit, left the cart, and called it a day.

The rest of the trip went off without a hitch, and we made it back to Watertown safely. The students again ran the program at the banquet with the three-foot trophy displayed on the table. When it was my turn to speak, I told the students that I asked them if they believed in magic last year, and they did, so for next year's trip they would have to use that magic to find Peter Pan's statue. The room was quiet, and a voice from the back of the room asked out loud, London? I said give that lady a prize, and the room exploded. I told the group to get their passports ready, because we were headed to London, England.

Peter Pan - a London landmark

London, England

The trip was all planned, and I was taking 55 students and 15 chaperones to London. After announcing the trip, one of the first things that I did was to go down to Mom's house and ask her if she would like to be a chaperone with us. Martha's Mom was 74 years young, and she had always dreamed of visiting London, but she thought her dream had passed her. I told her that the trip was on me.

The chaperones on the trip would be responsible for 4 students each. Each time I wanted to take roll, I would just say get with your chaperones and then ask the chaperones if they had their group. This was much easier than calling out everyone's name in an airport or anytime we were getting ready to move the group. We boarded a bus at the junior high and drove 100 miles to Sioux Falls to fly to Chicago. Once at the airport, Tish took the lead, and I was the last person in the rear. I felt like we were herding cattle leading so many people through the airport. Our flight out of Chicago to London was at 7:00 that evening. The flight would take almost 8 hours, and they were six hours ahead of us, so when we got to London, our bodies told us that it was two in the morning, although the time was 8:00 in the morning.

I did my homework on jet lag and knew that I had to keep the students up all day so that their bodies would adjust better to London time. So, we checked into our two hotels (because of the size of my group, we had to stay at two different hotels that were two blocks apart.) As a result, we were unfortunately treated like two separate groups the whole time we were in London. Once we put our luggage in the rooms, we ate breakfast and went on a walking tour of London. Our tour guide said Americans like to 'amble jam' across the street, which means they amble crossing the road on the yellow light and jam up the traffic, and Londoners hated that, but with 70 people in our group the last we did a lot of amble jamming.

We walked the students all day, and Mom was excitedly out-walking everyone in her group. We shut the day down at about 7:00 and sent the students to their hotel rooms. Martha and Cindy (Tish's girlfriend) were in charge of one hotel, and Tish and I were at the other hotel. The next day we would be performing at Victoria Gardens in the Victoria Embankment. I had my tux cleaned before we left home and much to my dismay when I pulled it out of the bag, I discovered that they did not put my pants with the jacket. One hour before showtime, I was in a department store trying to find a pair of black pants in size 33/29 (impossible). I got a pair of black jeans pants, so I could not wear my tux jacket. This time I *Improvised, Adapted,* and came up short.

We played over the noon hour, and there were lawn chairs set up in front of this beautiful outdoor stage. We had quite a program for them with selections including *A Handel Celebration, Thunder & Lightning Polka, Theme from Apollo 13, Asa's Lament* from Peer Gynt Suite, *Selections from Hook,* and we ended with *Stars and Stripes Forever.**

The orchestra got a nice standing ovation, and the students were beaming from ear to ear.

Concert at Victoria Embankment along the Thames

The next day I wanted the chaperones to have a little fun, so I took the group to Harrods, the most famous and largest department store in London. Some of the kids did not like it, but I had a fun afternoon planned. When the students came out of Harrods, over a third of them were proudly wearing "Doc Martin" boots, which were too spendy back in the States. That afternoon I took the students to Hamley's Toy Store, a world-renowned multi-story toy shop with events, demonstrations, and elaborate displays. They had a great time, and we almost ended on a perfect day.

All 70 of us took the tube (subway) to our restaurant. When you get off the tube, you walk around the circle underground until your street sign appears, and then you climb up the stairs to the street level. So, we found our sign and went up to the street. We walked another 5 blocks (amble jamming the whole way) to our restaurant. When we got to the restaurant, I called for roll call, and in a few seconds, 14 hands went up.

I counted again, and one student said, "Mr. Scales, my mom is not here."

We had lost a chaperone. My policy was if you got separated from the group, stay where you are, and I will find you. So, I ran the five blocks back to the tube, down to the inside circle, and down each stairway until I popped up on one street, and there she was. I walked toward her, and she turned to see me and just grabbed me for a second. She was so relieved to see me. We returned to the restaurant, and everyone was excited to see her.

The next day we played at Piccadilly Square, and I was more excited than the kids because this is where the opening scene of "My Fair Lady" starts (my favorite musical). After the performance, we had lunch at the Hard Rock Café of London (and you know I bought another "awful t-shirt"!)

We then spent the rest of the day at Madame Tussaud's Wax Museum, where my mother-in-law checked out the Fab Four.

The days were so exciting for the students, and every day I had something special planned for everyone. One day it was The Mousetrap, a murder mystery play by Agatha Christie, which opened in London's West End in 1952. According to Wikipedia, it ran continuously until March 16, 2020, when the stage performances had to be discontinued due to the COVID-19 pandemic. I was so proud of these South Dakota kids, and everyone from South Dakota would have been proud also, because they were great. They represented the United States with pride. The next day was a full one, and we set out for Salisbury Cathedral at 9:00 in the morning.

The bus rolled up on time, and I asked the driver to check on the other bus at the second hotel. He said they were ready to go, so we started for the Cathedral. We were 30 minutes down the road, and I asked the bus driver to check on the other bus (no cell phones). He had a phone but couldn't contact the other bus. He finally got them, and they were still at the hotel because the bus was late. So, we were forty-five minutes ahead of the other group for most of the morning because we had to stay on schedule. My group got to Salisbury Cathedral and had the opportunity to sit in on a sermon. The Cathedral was magnificent, and I wish that I could have changed places with Martha because they could not enter the church when her group got there. Our next stop was Bath, a community where the famous Roman Hot Spring Baths are still in existence, and this is where the other group finally caught up with us. Once we left Bath, we were headed to Stonehenge. This was 1997, and you could walk right up to the giant standing stones (about ten feet away) but now you cannot get within 50 yards of Stonehenge. We all got great pictures of this marvelous sight.

Stonehenge

The days were going by much too fast, but this particular day would prove to be an awesome one. We started the day by loading both buses and headed out to Hampton Court; it was an excellent ride, and we spent most of the day there. The grounds were enormous, and they had a giant hedge maze that most of the students got lost in. I enjoyed the kitchen because it was enormous, with room for everything.

Hampton Court

We had three more days left on this trip, and we flew out on the third day. I had not yet told the group about our next two days because I wanted it to be a surprise. When we got back to our hotel, I gave the students a little time to themselves, and I had some quiet time with Martha. She loved walking through English gardens, and that day she found the "Peter Pan" statue in Kensington Gardens.

The next day I gave all the chaperones the day off because it was a performance day for the orchestra, and I could manage the group alone. We were performing at Framlingham Castle, the summer home of Queen Mary (aka Bloody Mary.) The castle was now a private school, and the hall where we performed had the greatest acoustics that I had ever heard. The students could also hear the difference in this room, and they just filled it with sound. After the performance, we had a tour of the castle. What a great experience for the orchestra.

Our last night in London would be a magical night for the Youth Symphony. We experienced a live production of "Phantom of the Opera" in Her Majesty's Theatre, where it was first performed and still plays. The South Dakota students were dressed in their finest, and I was proud of their behavior for the last 11 days (but I expected nothing less of them).

This picture means so much to me. There are 70 people behind Martha and me walking down the street in London. I began thinking back to my 9th-grade English teacher at Gladstone, who told me, "Phil Scales, you will never amount to a hill of beans." (Yes, Eric W., they said that I was a lousy student also)

Well, I guess she was wrong. Every parent back home should be immensely proud of how the students represented the United States, because I sure was.

We were scheduled to fly out the next day, and now I had to deal with a situation that I had put on the back burner until now. A week before the trip, I got a call from one of the students. The student was a senior that lived out of town and took violin lessons from one of the private teachers in Watertown. She had been a part of the Youth Symphony for two years. Johanna's Mom wanted to give her a graduation present as an extension of the trip. She wanted her daughter to continue traveling in Europe when we left. I had a real problem with leaving a student behind, but her Mom said that she would be traveling with her aunt, who would arrive in London about 2 hours before we left the airport. I told Johanna that the three essential things that she had to protect were her violin, passport, and money. When we got to the airport and unloaded, we found out that Johanna did not have her violin (we never did find it). I got the students checked in, and I left Tish with the group as Martha and I took Johanna to her gate.

I was standing with her at the gate, and this young lady got off the plane, and I said to myself, gee, I hope this isn't her aunt, because this lady looks all of 18, but it was indeed her aunt, and she was 18 and had never traveled before. I did not know the next time that I would see Johanna because she was a senior and would not be at the banquet or in the group next year, so I thanked her for all her time with the Youth Symphony, and I hugged her. Johanna whispered in my ear - Mr. Scales, I'm scared. I told her just remember to keep track of her important things, like money and passport. As I walked away, I turned to Martha and said, "I'll never leave a student behind again."

We got home safely, and two days later, I got a call from Johanna's mother that the girls had their passports, IDs and all their money stolen. They were at the U.S. Embassy, and we had to get the Senator from South Dakota involved to get the girls back home. I vowed to never leave a student behind again.

Chapter Eight
Back to Competition and the Sea

After all of my planning for London, I started thinking of where we would go next year, so I kept my ears open, and I could hear the students talking about Florida again. I wanted the students to compete again, and the best competitions in the summer are in Florida. So, at the banquet, I announced to the students that we would be going to Disney for the competition. Then spent three days out to sea with stops in Key West, Cape Canaveral, and exploring Cocoa Beach. The students were excited about this competition because we were victorious the last time we went to Disney. The last time we played at Disney, the group wore Smurf blue shirts, but we were dressed in white tops, black bottoms, and red cummerbunds this year. The students were proud and ready to take the stage at Disney and performed magnificently. As I stood in front of these students, I felt a great sense of pride and was so thankful that I was allowed to work with such fine kids who believed in each other. I also looked down at my principal cello player and almost drew a tear because she was from Huron. She was one of my beginners when I continued that program in 1990. The Watertown Youth Symphony played with confidence and pride. When we finished playing, the audience gave us a warm welcome, and then we were off to the park until the Award Ceremony later in the day.

Once the students knew at the banquet that we were going to Disney again, they started to rebel against the Smurf blue shirts. So, this time we were at Disney in hunter-green shirts with black lettering. I had the same logo on the back (Mount Rushmore-Great Faces Great Places) and the same on the front (Watertown Area Youth Symphony). The students loved the new shirts, and it was fun spotting them throughout the park. Late that afternoon, we headed back for the Award Ceremony, and all the groups were excited to see how they fared. We won our second Superior Plus trophy, and the kids ran up to the stage to get the trophy.

I now had two trophies without a home because, as I said before, no business in Watertown ever supported the Youth Symphony and we had no place to display the trophies.

We stayed at Disney until the late-night fireworks show was over, and as we laid on the grass, I looked around at the students and thanked God for blessing me with such well-behaved kids. We then boarded the Carnival ship Dolphin for four days and three nights out to sea the following day. The only thing I had in mind was to spend some time with Martha and our son Michael, who was on his first Youth Symphony trip. When I moved to South Dakota, Michael was 18 months old, and now he was a fine violinist and standing tall.

Once we were all checked in on the ship, the students had the run of the ship without many rules, except no drinking or smoking allowed, just like any other school-sponsored event. Several hours into the cruise, I spotted Sue (not her real name) smoking with a group of guys that I did not know. I quietly reminded her of the rules, and she said she understood. A little later, I spotted Sue again smoking. I reminded her that she and her mom signed a letter giving me parental responsibility for her. If I caught her smoking again, I would confine her to her cabin. I was walking the deck, and who did I spot smoking again? I could not believe my eyes, and now the out-of-town people saw something that they had never seen before, Mr. Scales unleashed. I told Sue that she was confined to her cabin, and she asked for how long, and I asked her how long the trip was. I rounded up my female chaperones and told them that I wanted someone to visually check on Sue every 25 minutes.

Martha and the ladies had a schedule of who would check her cabin at different times. After a few hours, Sue asked to see me, and she apologized for her behavior, and I accepted it. Still, she had met this young man from Orlando, and after the cruise, she said that her mom would let her stay in Orlando to visit her uncle, whom she had never stayed with before. I said that her mom needed to call me, and she did. I told her mom that my responsibility was to bring everyone back home safely, and that's what I was going to do. Once Sue got home, she could send her back to Orlando if she wanted. I never mentioned Sue's behavior on the ship, but I had sworn that I would never leave a student behind, and I meant that with my whole heart. Sue came back to Watertown with me but never went back to Orlando.

The rest of the trip was nothing but fun, with a nice stop in Key West. The students loved Key West, and if I were there with just Martha, we would have hung out at Jimmy Buffett's famous Margaritaville Bar. The visit to Cape Canaveral was historical and a lot of fun. Our last stop at Cocoa Beach wasn't as fun because the white sand was too hot to walk on, so the kids spent a lot of time at the little mall. Our travels home were problem free, and the parents were excited at the banquet to see the fun pictures and hear the stories that the students had to tell. No one ever mentioned the Sue story, and that is good because my students know that I do not hold grudges and that what happens on that ship stays on that ship (or was that Vegas?!)

We now had two trophies, and who would have thought that four years ago? Now was the time to tell the students where we would be going next year, and I wanted this trip to be something they would always talk about and never forget. I told the kids that part of the trip would be a cruise, and I could hear a couple of moans because we had just come off a cruise. I said that I'll give you a few hints, and I started with the names Zeus, Hera, Athena, Apollo, Poseidon, and one parent said, "Oh my God, he's taking them to Greece."

She was right.

The Acropolis

I always tried to learn something from each trip that could help us on our future trips. The first time we went to the Bahamas, I did not give the students any background on the country, and I assumed they would check things out ahead of time, but I was wrong. On our first trip to the islands, one of the students said, "Mr. Scales, I had no idea that there were so many African Americans in Nassau, Bahamas."

I responded by saying that they were not African Americans but Bahamians. Every Black person is not an African American.

She then said, "Oh, I did not know that."

So, I wanted to make sure the students learned things about Greece on this trip before we departed.

The trip itinerary included places to visit in Athens such as the Acropolis, Parthenon, Temple of Olympian Zeus, National Archaeology Museum, and then a trip to Delphi. We would spend four days in Athens, then board a ship for a five-day tour of some of the Greece Islands, including Santorini, Mykonos, Patmos, Crete, Rhodes, and Kusadasi, Turkey. The students on the Youth Symphony trip had to learn three different currencies. In Stockholm, Sweden, it was the Swedish Krona, in London, it was the Euro, and in Greece, it would be the drachma. The drachma was the hardest to understand.

On the day of the trip, we loaded at the Middle School and drove 100 miles to Sioux Falls to get our flight to St. Louis. We had an excellent layover, and we boarded our 7:00 flight to Athens. The trip would take 12 hours. We had three meals on the flight, and I enjoyed the flight, but a few students and Martha got airsick. When we reached Athens, our bodies told us that it was 7:00 in the morning, but in Athens, it was 3:00 in the afternoon, and it was hot. We arrived at the hotel at 4:00, and I went into the hotel first and told them who I was and that I represented the Watertown Youth Symphony.

The lady at the desk said, "You are the boss."

And I replied yes. She then said that I would get a unique room. Martha and I were the only ones in the group with an air-conditioned room, and I loved being the "boss" for the next four days because it was really hot outside. We also had a balcony that directly faced the Parthenon.

The students went on a walking tour as soon as we got to the hotel and we walked for a couple of hours, because in Greece in the summer people eat a very late dinner. This also would help with the jet lag that the students would endure. Our first dinner was terrific, and so were the Greek people. The waiter and waitress would bring our food, and every five minutes, they would dance as a group to Greek music. They would dance all the while shouting *Opa!* which means good cheer. The waiters would grab one of the students and pull them onto the dance floor, shouting *Opa!* Soon, all the students were on the dance floor dancing and shouting *Opa!* I watched the students have a great time, and before I knew it, I was on the dance floor shouting *Opa!* as well. It was a 2-hour dinner, and it had been a great day.

Opa!

When we got back to the hotel, I hit the AC button and was glad to be the Leader. The next few days would be jam-packed. We listened to history lessons, and we had an excellent tour guide, so the language was never a problem. If someone spoke to me, I didn't worry about not understanding the Greek language, because the people were so amiable. This trip was memorable because I had my two oldest sons, Michael and Jason, along. We went to the site where they held the first Olympics, and I ran around the track with my sons and a few other students. We took a tour up to Delphi, driving through the winding mountain roads. On the way back, we stopped at a Greek restaurant in the mountains and had an excellent spaghetti lunch with a Greek salad. I fell in love with Greek tomatoes and could eat them all day.

Temple of Apollo at Delphi

The next day we hit the spot that Martha had been waiting for - the Acropolis. The monuments are universal symbols of the classical spirit and civilization and form the most significant architectural and artistic complex bequeathed by Greek Antiquity (Wikipedia). The day was beautiful (a little hot), and I had fun just watching everyone have a good time. They had a gift shop, and the guys fell in love with Greek letter openers styled as long daggers almost 8 inches long. I told them that they would have to put those in their big suitcases going back home (but did they listen to me?) On our last day in Athens, we spent time in the National Archaeology Museum and in the afternoon visited the Temple of Poseidon, which perches high above the Aegean Sea on Cape Sounion.

The following day, we packed all our belongings and headed for the cruise ship for our five-day excursion to the Greek Islands. Our first island was the beautiful city of Santorini, which is one of the Cyclades islands in the Aegean Sea. Santorini had been devastated by a volcanic eruption in the 16th century BC. To get from the port to the top of Santorini, you have two transfer options, cable car or donkey ride. The donkey rides took 35 minutes, and most of the students took the donkey ride, and so did my whole family. We were in Santorini for four hours during the day, but how I wished for one night with dinner in this beautiful city with my lovely wife. Our next island was Mykonos, it was known for its summer atmosphere and all-night parties. We reached Mykonos mid-day, and we had lunch on the island, but all I wanted to do was sit at a table by the sea and share a bottle of wine with Martha.

Little Venice on Mykonos

The urge was so overwhelming that I turned to Martha and promised her that I would bring her back to this spot on our 25th wedding anniversary (we were at 17 years at that point), and I did. The nights on the cruise ship floating on the Aegean Sea were unbelievable. Sitting and watching the students look out upon the sunset and realizing that they were a long way from South Dakota overwhelmed me.

Mykonos Windmills

The next day was an early departure from the ship at 9:00 am to the island of Patmos, and I gave the students an option - if you were going with me to Patmos, be at the gate at 8:30. If not, have a good sleep in, and I'll have a headcount at noon; any chaperone left on the ship will be in charge until I get back. The following day, Martha, Tish, Cindy, five students, and I got off the boat. Patmos was famous for its religious past. This is the island where Saint John the Theologian wrote the Book of Revelation (the Apocalypse.) In St. John's cave, you could see the imprint of his hand on the stone he leaned on while writing Revelations. I had a strange sensation run through me as I put my hand in St. John's handprint.

Harbor in Rhodes

I wish that I had played Dad and made my boys come, but the option was the kids' choice, and they were students first. The next day we had a noon stop at the island of Rhodes. This was the largest of Greece's Dodecanese islands. It was known for its beach resorts, ancient ruins, and remnants of its occupation by the Knights of St. John during the Crusades. I told everyone to meet at the café on the main departing floor, and we would leave from there. As the students were waiting in the closed café, the officers on that floor closed the café doors, so we had to wait outside the café.

At noon I told the students to get with their chaperones so I could take a quick headcount. I saw that one chaperone had a missing student and I had informed the group that if you missed a departure time, you stayed on the ship. We would deal with it when everyone got back. You could hear a little muttering between the students, and then I said, let's go, and we headed off the ship. As we left the boat, I could feel two eyeballs burning into the back of my head, and I knew it was Martha, because I had just left our son on the ship.

We went down to the beach where you could see two giant statues of the Crusaders, and we laid out as a group. Still, it wasn't long before we noticed that some of the people at the beach were sunbathing topless. The guys were a little uneasy, so they ran out and swam to a pier that was about seventy yards out. I watched as they swam out to the dock, and they quickly turned and swam back. When they reached the group, I asked them what had happened, and they said that everyone on the pier was nude.

After the beach, we walked through the Old Town featuring the medieval Streets of the Knights and the Palace of the Grand Masters. We were off the ship for about 2 ½ hours, and the students wanted to get back and eat, so we came back early. Once back on board the vessel Martha and I went to Michael's room. He felt terrible for disappointing us but said that he was the first student in the café and laid down in the back and went to sleep, but when he woke up, everyone was gone, and he was locked in. We had two hours before we would leave, so Martha took Michael for a private tour of Rhodes. He ended up seeing more than the group because Martha skipped the beach. I never had a student late again for anything else on the trip because I guess the students realized that if I would leave my oldest son, I would not hesitate to leave them. My thinking was that I was the Leader first and then the husband and father. That philosophy worked for King Arthur and Guinevere, but sadly it did not work at all for Phil Scales (just ask Martha!)

The next day we spent time on the island of Crete and visited Knossos, the largest Bronze Age archaeological site on Crete and possibly Europe's oldest city. The Palace of Knossos is a monumental symbol of Minoan civilization. Our last stop was the port of Kusadasi in Turkey. Kusadasi is a beach resort town on Turkey's western Aegean coast. Its seafront promenade, marina, and harbor are lined with hotels and restaurants.

The shopkeepers here were genuinely friendly. I bought a Greek key necklace for Martha, and after the transaction, the owner brought out a little pot of hot apple tea, and we drank hot tea to honor the deal. At noon, every shop owner (all men) would come out of their shop and kneel on their carpet to pray to Allah. It was an impressive sight.

It was time to return home, and we were at the airport for our flight to New York's LaGuardia Airport and then to St. Louis, the last leg to Minneapolis, followed by a four-hour bus ride back to Watertown. So, we spent a lot of time reflecting on our great adventures in Greece. The flight took 13 hours to get to New York, and we had a three-hour layover there. As the students were going through the metal detectors for baggage check, I heard a commotion in front of me. I could see that the belt checker had four of our boys in front of her and was lecturing them. So, I went over to see what was going on, and I could see that she had the boys' dagger/letter openers in front of them (this was before 9/11). She asked the boys how dare they attempt to bring these items on the plane. She talked so loudly that ten of the other guys who had already passed the check-in came back and gave her their daggers/letter openers. So now 14 daggers/letter openers were sitting in front of her, and she was irate.

I apologized for the guys not putting the items in their big suitcases, but I always carried my briefcase with me, and I offered to put the letter openers in it and lock the briefcase while on the plane. She went along with that because she knew that I would never open that briefcase and pass out the daggers! It would have been an entirely different situation if this had occurred after 9/11.

As we sat at our gate, I got a call to come up to the front desk. The clerk at the desk told me that our connecting flight from Detroit was caught in a storm and that we could not get out until the next day. I explained to the clerk that we had to make that St. Louis flight. We had a chartered bus waiting for us in Minneapolis tonight, and I had no way of contacting their parents at this short notice. The clerk said she could not help me, so I asked her to speak to her supervisor. The supervisor came and talked with me, but I was getting nowhere with him, so I asked to speak to his supervisor. This time, his supervisor asked me what I would like them to do about the situation. I said I would like him to call St. Louis and see if they would hold that plane until my students could make that flight. She agreed to call the St. Louis airport to see if they would keep that plane on the ground until we could get there. I was called to the desk, and they informed me that St. Louis would hold the 7:30 flight on the ground until we got there. We finally got on the flight out of New York, and when we hit the ground, they had people running us to our flight that was being held on our behalf.

I was the last one on the plane, and the people already on the plane did not look happy. As my butt hit my seat, the plane door slammed, and I looked at my watch, and it was 11:30 pm. Those poor people had been sitting on this plane since 7:00. I turned to Martha and said, "Our luggage did not make this flight," and I was right.

When we got to Minneapolis, we had to find someone to take descriptions of the students' bags and get directions to their homes because now they had to deliver the bags to the kids' homes in South Dakota.

As tired as we were, this was the funniest part of the trip, listening to students' directions to their houses. Example: Make a right off the highway on county road AA, drive five miles, turn at the big oak tree on the right, go another mile, left turn at the red barn, but if you crossed the bridge, you went too far. Once you pass the red barn, count seven mailboxes, and we are 100 yards past that on the left. The looks on the baggage handlers' faces were priceless. We had a great banquet, and the students' stories were terrific. This is genuinely one trip they will never forget. I announced our upcoming trip, but I'll save this story for later, and instead return to 1992.

In the fall of '92, I had over 100 string players in the junior high orchestra. I wanted the orchestra to play full orchestra literature. Still, I would have to get permission from the band teacher because we would have to bring in the wind players from her band. This did not go over very well with the band director. Still, now in '92, this made perfect sense because with both the Youth Symphony and the Watertown Symphony starting, it would be great to get our local wind players involved. She said no, so I went to the principal, and fortunately, he liked the idea, so we set it up where I could get wind players out of class once a week to work on full orchestra music. I then had over 130 students in my junior high full orchestra, and it was the largest in the State.

ALL STATE ORCHESTRA — Sixteen students at Watertown Senior High School were named to the All-State Orchestra. The orchestra will perform at 8 p.m. Saturday, Nov. 7, in the Rushmore Plaza Civic Center Arena in Rapid City. From left are front: Jessica Witcher, Jo Ann Falk, Melissa Moses, Carolyn Bue, Kristi Corey, Wendy Determan and Amy Brekke; back: Andy Brandlee, Heidi Dohrer, Michelle Monteith, Brandi DeWall, Joe Brunick, Laura Ford, Rob Lubbers, Jennifer Redli and Paul Determan. (Public Opinion photo by Scott Carbonneau)

Kristi Corey. Heidi Dohrer, Melissa Moses

I almost had to put earplugs in to shut out all the negativity about the Watertown Symphony being started, but I continued to move forward. Our first concert was 2 ½ months away, and people could not imagine what the first concert would be like, except for the orchestra members. We were putting together an intense opening concert, and I wanted to make a statement. I wanted each concert to be an event, so I got our local Hy-Vee store to donate veggies, cheese, and meat platters. They also presented a cake for our special opening. We had over 500 people sitting in the audience in our opening concert. The first number on the program was the *Zampa Overture*. I wanted our first number to start out with high energy and showcase the violin sections. You can't have a good orchestra without the best horses up front, and I had an excellent violin section. Five awesome violin themes flow throughout *Zampa*, and the violins had a ball in rehearsals with this piece.

The *Gayane-Ballet Suite* was a number that showcased the woodwinds, brass, and percussion section. *Danse Macabre* was eminently suitable for this Halloween concert, and it gave the concertmaster a chance to show his talents. The last number, Beethoven's *Symphony Number 1*, was all for me. I know it's not a number most conductors end a concert on, but I wanted the audience to see a black man (who was "just" a junior high conductor, and who most said could not pull this off), directing Beethoven.

The audience was seated, and the orchestra members were on stage, so I tapped my right pocket for Mr. Stone, said "Do it Now," and quickly walked on stage. I stepped on my podium and looked over to Martha, sitting at the second violin stand on the outside. Then I looked at the 4th first violin stand at the girl on the outside, because she was a junior in high school and has been one of my top students since starting with me in 4th grade. The baton went up, and the Watertown Symphony made its debut. (You can watch and listen to each one of these songs on my YouTube channel—Conductor Phil Scales)

After the concert, when I took my last bow, I did what I always do after conducting. I stood in the hallway, shook every player's hand, and thanked them for the music they just gave me. Then I would stand and greet everyone who came to the reception in the cafeteria. The next day at school, not one teacher said anything about the concert because none of them went, but there was a good article in the paper about the show. Later that morning, I got a phone call that changed my outlook. The call was from Vera Way Marghab, and she called to tell me how impressed she was with the concert and thanked me for standing tall when I could have just not tried at all. Ms. Marghab and I would become music friends, and I would later do a concert to honor her work.

The week before this concert, I was in Aberdeen, South Dakota, for All-State Orchestra. I had several 9th graders make the orchestra. At the directors' meeting, I was elected President of ASTA (American String Teachers Association) for the next 2 years. I was the first Black president ever in South Dakota. In the coming year, I would represent SD at the National Convention in Ann Arbor, Michigan.

This turned out to be a great trip because I had the chance to hang out with my old roommate, Ike Brown, who lived in Detroit. The last time I saw Ike was at my first wedding in the summer of '75 (he was my best man). So that was a long time ago, but we made up for the lost time. The years were going fast with all the concerts I had lined up for my groups. In December, I had a Youth Symphony concert, a junior high-grade school tour, a junior high full orchestra concert with 130 students, and a Christmas concert for the Watertown Symphony Orchestra. At the Christmas concert, I pulled together four of the finest voices in Watertown; Mary (junior high vocal teacher), the high school band teacher, his wife, and the male high school vocal teacher. They sang Chip Davis's *Christmas Traditions* by candlelight, and we also played Mannheim Steamroller's *Stille Nacht* and Leroy

Anderson's *Christmas Festival.*

It's now the beginning of 1993, and I'm preparing for my next Watertown Symphony concert in March. I started the Watertown Symphony at a higher level than I did with the Huron Symphony. The Huron Symphony took me three years before I brought in a guest artist. This was only our third concert with Watertown, and I brought in a professional pianist, Pierce Emata. He played Ravel's *Piano Concerto for the Left Hand.* Pierce later performed with the Huron Symphony and played Grieg's *Piano Concerto in A minor** (all musical selections marked with an * can be heard on my YouTube channel—Conductor Phil Scales). We also played *English Folk Song Suite* by Ralph Vaughan Williams and Mendelssohn's *Symphony No. 5* (*movements 2-4*).*

ALL-STATE ORCHESTRA — These Watertown musicians will play in the All-State Orchestra this Saturday. Left to right in the front row: JoAnn Falk, Laura Ford, Carolyn Bue. Middle row: Jessica Smith, Jana Taken, Kristi Corey, Jessica Witcher, Heidi Dohrer, Amy Brekke. Back row: Joel Brunick, Michelle Monteith, Jennifer Redlin, Andy Brandlee, Marla Freesemann and Paul Determan. The All-State Orchestra and Chorus concert will be Saturday at 8 p.m. at the Barnett Center in Aberdeen. Tickets are available at the center's ticket office and are $5 for adults and $3 for students. (Public Opinion photo by Jason Nordmark)

All-State Orchestra: 10 of these students were my private students

Joel Brunick, Jessica Witcher, Andy Brandlee

With Nadia adjusting positively to life in Watertown, things were finally shaping out on the home front. She seemed to be having more fun at home and school. Nadia was on the 7th-grade track team, and she had my speed, so it was fun to see her flying past everyone. Tashai was on the 8th-grade track team, and I found a way to make all their track meets. The deal that I had with her mom was for Nadia to stay a year with me, then we would see how her behavior was, and we would decide at that point on our next move. I told her mom that she was doing great, but her mom wanted her home now. It was April, and she only had two months of school left and I asked Carell not to pull her out until after school. Then she could just stay because she would be back for the summer. She refused, and Nadia had to return to Florida in April, and none of the girls came that summer or the next several summers. My hunch was that they were afraid that the girls might ask to stay with me once they got back to Watertown. I could be wrong, but there was always an excuse for why the girls could not come.

My goal for my symphonies was to be an innovator in the industry. I wanted to do things that were not being done at that time. One of the things that I did with the Watertown Symphony was to highlight the famous people in our town. One of those people was Vera Way Marghab, and the other was our own renowned national artist, Terry Redlin. I had Ms. Marghab (linens) and Mr. Redlin (paintings) display their works in the hallway outside the auditorium before the concert.

The orchestra played *Pictures at an Exhibition**. After the show at the reception, Ms. Marghab and her brother Kenny Way (who owned the newspaper) thanked me again for the Watertown Symphony. To be an innovator, I played a piece by John Williams, which was the last 13 minutes of E.T. (the bicycle scene). When we played it, I had two 50-inch screen TVs in front of the stage and a small monitor on my conductor's stand so I could direct the action. The orchestra could not see the film, so they had to watch my conducting closely. The audience of over 1000 people enjoyed the movie set to live music, as well as Indiana Jones and Apollo 13.

The hardest part for me in E.T. was having the horns hit the "rainbow" in E.T. right on time, and we nailed it. The splicing of the other two films took hours, but it was so much fun after the project was finished, and the audience loved it. We also performed Michael Flatley's *Lord of the Dance* with 20 dancers on stage. My children's concerts were always a big hit and would draw between 1000 and 1200 students each time.

Our most significant concert draw was when we performed the *Messiah** (Christmas version) in Huron. We also performed it in the gym in Watertown (the Easter version) because it could hold up to 4,000 people. I also have the Hallelujah Chorus from the Huron Symphony on my YouTube channel.

One of the first soloists who played with the Watertown Symphony was a young clarinet player, Ani Berberian. She attended SDSU in Brookings, South Dakota, and later played clarinet in the U.S. Air Force Band. I hoped that the music teachers in town would help promote this concert for young students, but they did not, and we had under 350 people at the concert. It was a shame that more students did not come to this event. Ani played *Clarinet Concerto No. 1 in f minor* by Weber. You can see all three movements on my YouTube channel-Conductor Phil Scales. The white-haired violinist sitting next to Ani in the video was her dad, Hratch Berberian, who was a string teacher at SDSU for many years and a dear friend.

Chapter Nine
Middle School

In 1994 Watertown Junior high was turned into Watertown middle school. Still, it was not a traditional middle school because a conventional middle school is from 6th grade to 8th grade, but our middle -school was only 7th and 8th grade. All the other middle schools in the State were 6th-8th grade except Watertown. This setup changed a few things because I would no longer have the 9th graders go to music contests or help prepare them for All-State. After this change, our numbers in All-State dropped rapidly. The high school orchestra now had over a hundred players, broken down into three orchestras. They played very few full orchestra pieces in the top group, and the other two orchestras never played any full orchestra pieces.

I still had 85 students at the middle school and another 55 in 6th grade. So, I started an honors 6th-grade orchestra. We would meet two days a week after school at the middle school so that I could keep them moving in the same direction as my middle-school players. My teaching style had not changed because now my 8th graders had become the orchestra's leaders. With my 6th graders meeting twice a week, they would learn the leadership skills needed to play in middle school. This did help with space in the music department at the middle school. This also cut down on the number of students leaving out of class for lessons, which the staff really liked. Some people thought I had some spare time because the head basketball coach gave me a call to coach 6th-grade basketball.

I played a lot of basketball in my spare time, and I played with Kraig, who was the head coach, many times. I took the position because the next year, I would have a chance to coach my son Michael, who was a good player. Michael played on a traveling basketball team since third grade. I would have practice from 3:30 to 4:45, and games would run from 3:45 to 4:45. On Mondays I would then drive home, shower, get back in the van (with Art and sometimes with students with me), and drive to Huron for our symphony rehearsals. I did this for eleven years.

I felt terrible for the ninth graders because the high school teacher didn't put in the time to prepare them for All-State. They did not play at the music contest anymore because she only took the top group to the competition. The one thing that the students noticed right away was how they were judged at the high school level. If you took private lessons from Mr. Scales, you sat in the back of your section, which was very noticeable. I had a ninth grader taking classes from me, and I entered him for All-State auditions. When the list came out from the high school director, his name was not on the list.

When I got to the All-State rehearsal in Aberdeen, SD, I checked the orchestra list, and his name was on it. I questioned the high school director, and she said that she had forgotten to put his name on her list. I called my student, Trevor, and his parents drove him 100 miles to the first rehearsal. This practice of treating the students differently went on for another five years until my son hit the high school orchestra.

The school year was wrapping up, and my Youth Symphony was headed to Stockholm, Sweden. On May 22, 1995, I heard that Ms. Vera Way Marghab had passed away. It was unfortunate news because she was such a lovely lady, and I enjoyed our talks about music. I got a call later that summer from the Watertown Foundation, and they said that Ms. Marghab had left money for all the Art programs in Watertown.

The town of Watertown was rich in the arts. We had several artists, an acting group called the Town Players, a municipal band, a local chorus, and a female music group. The Watertown Foundation president told me they needed the organizations to get together, share their budgets, and list things to keep their organizations moving forward. After I was given all the information, I was told that they wanted me to be the arts facilitator of this group and pull everyone together.

This was a shock for me because I did not have a lot of support from several organizations, and I did not know what to expect. In the first meeting, I had the group select a board to sit and make decisions with me that would be suitable for the overall organization. We had two sessions, and I thought the meetings went well until I started getting hate mail. I told Martha that I did not need this, so I took the letters to my board at the next meeting and said I thought it would be best to resign.

The board would not hear it and said they wanted me to stay, so I did. When we finished the project, every organization received a nice chunk of money. It would receive money each year, with the understanding you would turn your remaining assets back to the Watertown Foundation if your organization ever went under. I was glad that I stayed because I think Ms. Marghab wanted me to be the facilitator, and I miss her.

I was starting my sixth year with the Huron Symphony and my third with the Watertown Symphony, with concerts in two months. One of the main pieces that we would play at Huron would be the *Romeo & Juliet Fantasy**. This was a work that required the orchestra to play with passion, excitement, and energy. This was a piece that I genuinely enjoyed conducting, and I did so with a lot of passion. In Watertown, we would be playing *The New World Symphony,* which we were performing a lot earlier than I did with the Huron Symphony.

The fall season was moving relatively quickly; it was October 3, 1995, and I was going home for lunch with Martha. This was the day that everyone was glued to the T.V. screen, because it was the day the verdict came in for O.J. Simpson, who was charged with killing his former wife, Nicole Simpson Brown. When they found her body (June 12, 1994), my Youth Symphony was on our way back from our first cruise, and we watched the story unfold at a McDonald's.

Martha and I watched the verdict, and like everyone else, we had our own opinions. I went back to school, and as I got close to the teacher's lounge, I could hear a lot of noise coming from the teachers' lounge from the hallway. I opened the door and walked in, and everyone stopped talking. In fact, it was so quiet that you could hear a feather hit the floor. I felt like a fly in a bowl of white milk. I walked over to my mailbox, got my mail, and walked straight out of the room. No one said a word because everyone thought I was rooting for O.J. Simpson. After all, I was black, and every black person wanted to see the Juice go free, is what they were thinking. (Remember, Watertown only had two Black men in a town of 20,000).

This felt like a racist mentality to me, and for the first time since I'd been in Watertown, I felt a sense of fear. I went to my office and called Martha, and we talked for a while. I could not understand that these were the same teachers who had "Tolerance" stickers on their doors. I never got any response from the teachers in the lounge, and I had been in town for 9 years at that point.

Curriculum on the Wall

The school systems that I had been associated with were always trying to find the perfect teaching design for students. I had worked with the Madeline Hunter system, the Boys Town Model, and now Curriculum on the Wall. When they announced that we would be doing this education model, I just thought that it was something that would not apply to music, but I was so wrong. With the Curriculum on the Wall, I could list everything that a student should know and be able to play; I could show parents exactly where their students were on the chart; and a student could see what it took to advance to the top groups.

The whole music staff worked on the Curriculum on the Wall together, and it was a battle the entire time. I taught all the violins and the violas in grade school, and the high school teacher taught the cellos and basses. Our ideas of where the students should be each year were day and night. I always felt that the cellos and basses were always behind the upper strings, but once they got to middle school, I could try and catch them up to where I felt they should be.

My students liked the new education model. I was ahead of most teachers because I was already doing some of these steps. If a parent had concerns about a student's placement or grade in my class, I could show them what the kids could and could not do by showing the grade level objectives on the wall chart.

The Harlem Globetrotters

I started coaching sixth-grade basketball, and I was excited to get back into coaching sports. When I was growing up the sport that I did the least was basketball. I played on the 8th and 9th-grade teams but could not find the time to perfect my skills. I could play, but at 5'6" how far was I going to go? So, I honed my football, baseball, and music skills.

The head basketball coach at Watertown invited the Harlem Globetrotters to Watertown to play against all the basketball coaches, and I was one of them. I was so excited to be playing with the Globetrotters and made a shot that I will never forget. I was at the corner of the foul line with my back to the hoop, and Meadowlark

Lemon was guarding me. Meadowlark had just come back to the Trotters that year.

I took a pass, faked a hard right, spun back to the left with a 15-foot skyhook, and hit nothing but the bottom of the net. The crowd went wild, but Meadowlark did not, and I became that "guy." He was the person that all the tricks were played on, the one that they would dribble circles around, bounce the ball between his legs, bounce the ball off his head, and yes, get his pants pulled down. I should have missed the shot. There were over 5,000 people at the game, but that was not unusual for Watertown basketball. They filled the stands every Friday night with five to six thousand people.

My Friday nights were always spent with my family, and we spent a lot of time at the games until two incidents stopped my family from going. The first was when the Sisseton basketball team and cheerleaders came to play the Watertown Arrows. I went to the game to support and cheer for the Sisseton team because I had a lot of Sisseton band players in my Youth Symphony and Tish taught in Sisseton. The town of Sisseton sits on part of the Indian reservation. Their cheerleaders were mainly Native American, and they were a class C school. Watertown was a class A school, so they were already out of their league.

During the game, some of the students from Watertown started making Indian calls to the Sisseton cheerleaders, and they began to throw water balloons at them. The girls ran off the floor in tears, and my family and I left the game. I reported this to the Athletic Director the next day, but nothing happened.

A few games later, Yankton High school came to Watertown (a division rival). They had a Black player who was 6'7" and an outstanding player, so good that near the end of the game, some people in the stands started shouting, "Get the N (the N-word) off the court."

This young man shut everyone up by stealing the ball and slamming the ball down through the net. He got a technical call against him because dunking was not allowed during this time in high school basketball, but it did not matter because his point was made. I never took my family to another high school basketball game.

The grade school that I coached at was my neighborhood school, and my boys were in 5th and 4th grade, so I had another year before I would coach my son Jason. I tried to get the young kids in the neighborhood to be involved in school activities other than music and sports, so I started a chess club at my kids' grade school. I taught my boys how to play the game, but they needed other people who could play too, so I formed a chess club, and I had 12 kids sign up to learn how to play.

I had to change around some of my private lesson students to fit in the chess club time. We hit the ground running, and we got so good that we involved other grade schools, and we had running chess leagues within the grade schools. The sixth-grade basketball league were the same kids and parents involved in little league baseball; need I say more? We had a zero-tolerance policy with parents about shouting or degrading an official, player, or coach. We also had a 20-point lead rule where you would then shut off the scoreboard. The six-grade program was to be a learning league and not embarrass any player. The coach at the home court gym had to be the game's official. (Just him). This was difficult for me because I would coach both teams on the floor. If the players on both teams were committing the same foul, I would stop the game, pull both groups together and explain why I was calling the foul.

Some parents hated seeing this, but sixth-grade basketball was a teaching level, and I wanted all the players to do well; it was not about winning. I remember one game where a parent kept yelling at the kids and the official, so I reminded the parent of our zero-tolerance policy. Still, he kept going at it, so I asked him to leave, and he came onto the court, but eventually he did leave.

After the game, his wife came up to me and said, "Do you know who I am?"

She was an attorney in Watertown and was also on the Watertown Foundation and signed the checks from the money that Ms. Marghab left the Symphony.

I said, "I know who you are."

And she replied, "Remember that the next concert."

After my first season with sixth graders, I now knew that if you wanted to coach this age of kids, then they had better be orphans.

Mount Marty College

The city of Watertown, with its 20,000 people (two Black men), had a college in town, and I was a professor there for several years, teaching music classes in the evening. I really enjoyed teaching at this level, and sometimes I would have a teacher from the middle school in my class, and some did not like it, but I was the professor. Mount Marty College held their graduations without any music because they did not have a music department. Hence, one day I offered the Youth Symphony to perform the music for the graduation.

They asked what we could do, and I told them we could do the whole program for them. This was the first time Mount Marty's graduates ever had any live music with their graduations, and they loved it. The administration and family members were really impressed with the group. The Youth Symphony was planning for our first competition at Disney World, and I received a beautiful letter from Mount Marty with a nice-sized check enclosed. The check was enough to pay for the chartered buses to take the students to and from the Sioux Falls Airport. I never asked for any payment; I just thought it would add more class to the graduation.

The string numbers in the grade school continued to grow, so much so that we hired a part-time string instructor for the grade schools. With so many new students we needed bigger classrooms. When I first started to teach in Watertown, we would have classes in the boiler room, on stage, gym, in hallways, in the nurse's office, or in the principal's office. Still, with so many kids, we now needed an entire room. We had over 200 string players in the grade school, 85 in grades 7th & 8th, and 90 in the high school. The school year of '96-97 went well, and it was a fun year. I had the opportunity to coach my son Michael in basketball. He was a good player and a great student, and I worked with Martha again, who had been hired as the part-time string teacher.

State Music Convention

The school year '97-98 was starting, and I had 85 string students in 7th & 8th grade and got an invitation to play at the State Music convention again. The convention wasn't until February 12, 1998, which gave me plenty of time to do something out of the ordinary for a middle-school orchestra. The vocal teachers in the elementary schools of Watertown were working on Orff instruments with their students, so I ordered a string piece that was written for Orff instruments and strings. We performed the music with 85 string players and 20 Orff instruments. (This concert is on my YouTube

Channel-Conductor Phil Scales). This was a fun concert for me because I had my two oldest sons playing in the orchestra, one on violin and the other on cello. When I moved to Watertown, the boys were 18 months and 5 months old, so they grew into the program.

The Bush Fellowship

In the fall of '98, I received a letter from the Bush Fellowship saying that someone had nominated me for a Fellowship. I filled out the questionnaire and sent it back to them. There were over 800 applicants who were trying for the awards, and they would have six finalists meet in Minneapolis in the spring. As a Fellow candidate, you had to go around the State to have interviews with board members, and they would decide if you continued or not. So, after each interview, you had to wait to get a letter in the mail to see if you would move on. I had to have my program set up and ready to go if I made the finals. My project was to get a Master's in art administration. (I already had my Master's in the Administration of Education).) I would earn it in a college in London, England; it would be a two-year program. This meant that I would be uprooting my family for two years, and I had to be accepted into a school in London by that spring. The school that I applied to was the Birbeck School of the Arts at the University of London.

One Saturday morning at 5:30 a.m. the phone rang, and it was an official from the Birbeck School of the Arts, who wanted to do an interview with me. The person doing the interview must have forgotten about the time difference because it was 11:30 in the morning there. Still, we did an hour interview, and I got a letter in the mail a few days later that I had been accepted to the Birbeck School of the Arts.

I did five interviews for the Fellowship and made it to the final six. In Minneapolis that spring (1999), we all met at Oak Ridge Hotel and Conference Center in Chaska, MN. I enjoyed spending time with the finalists and attending the leadership classes that we had for four days. Still, the evenings got a little longer because we had to spend time talking to all the people involved with selecting the winners.

The judges would walk up to you and say, well, Phil tell me about yourself. It got to the point where I wanted to just throw up on my shoes when someone would ask me to tell them about myself. The

142

weekend ended with each finalist getting five minutes to sell their program to the judges. The two winners would get a call on Monday at noon. I was in class that Monday morning, and around 10:00, I got a call from the office that I had an important phone call. The call was from the secretary of the Bush Fellowship, and she said that the judges wanted to know if I could cut my program down to eighteen months. I told her that I did not think I could finish the program in that short time. She thanked me, and I got a phone call at 1:00 that I had been one of the top three, but they only selected two. She said they wanted me to know. I told Martha, and we both cried because we had worked so hard to get to that final point. I did win Middle-School Teacher of the Year a few weeks later, which meant a great deal to me.

A Dream Becomes a Reality

The summer of '99 had started. I ran into a friend named Johnny Cavelle, who operated three dance studios in South Dakota, in Watertown, Aberdeen, and Huron. My daughter, who was in third grade, and my youngest son, in fourth, were both in Johnny's dance studio. I had worked with Johnny two years prior when we performed the Nutcracker Dance Suite for Christmas concerts in Huron and Watertown. The shows were a huge success, and we had over 1200 people at each concert. So, this day Johnny and I sat down for coffee and started to talk about doing the whole Nutcracker Ballet. We both were excited about putting something like this together and started planning how we would do it. I told Johnny that I could write a few grants and set up the three performance sites. Also, I would take care of any legal matters that might arise.

Johnny would organize the dancers and hire the choreographer and the two professional dancers. We both would help manage the stage setting and make the costumes. I would take care of the publicity and all the incoming bills that we would incur. When Johnny and I left the meeting, the *Nutcracker Ballet* was set for December of 1999. I was excited to get started on the details of putting on such a project.

I first had to reserve three places to perform, one in Aberdeen and Huron and two performances in Watertown. The dates would be December 3rd, 4th, and two performances in Watertown on the 5th. I then had to sell the program to the two boards I was responsible for (Huron & Watertown).

The challenging hurdle was ordering the three backdrops for the *Nutcracker's* three-act performance - the party scene, a forest in winter, and the Land of the Sweets. I had them reserved for me coming out of Los Angeles on December 2nd, a night before our first performance. So, the first time we would have them would be the night of the first performance in Aberdeen. This was cutting it close, but it was the best I could do because most people doing the *Nutcracker* had the backdrops reserved for a year or two out from their concert date. We were just getting started, but I did have them booked. I had the music ordered, and I had the first full rehearsal set with the dancers for the day after Thanksgiving. I had all of this planned before our first rehearsal, the first week in September.

In August, I had my meetings with my board members. We struggled with what the price of tickets should be because they were thinking of the performance at a high school level. My goal was to take this group to a higher level than they could imagine, because I knew what Johnny would bring to the table, and we would match that level. The board wanted five-dollar tickets, but I got them to agree to twenty-dollar tickets for everyone because that is what it would take to meet our budget.

My two youngest kids got letters from Johnny with all the information about this excellent opportunity to perform the *Nutcracker* with a live orchestra, and how excited he was to work with me. The auditions would start the first week of August, and then it would be three full months of just nothing but *Nutcracker* rehearsal for his students.

The next four months would be hard because I still had Symphony concerts in October for Huron and Watertown. The All-State Orchestra was the first week of November. My oldest son Michael would be auditioning because he was in 9th grade. I also had the planning to do for the next summer's Youth Symphony trip, which would be taking them out to the Eastern sea coast of the United States.

A Huge Decision to Make

I got a call from Johnny four days before the start of the dance auditions, and he said that his mom had become extremely ill and that he could not focus on the *Nutcracker* at this time. He said he was profoundly sorry but knew that he could not handle the extra pressure of dealing with the

Nutcracker and his mom's health. I told him that I understood and would take the necessary steps to cancel the show. We had everything in place to start the project. The professional dancers were hired, and the choreographers were already in town. So, I began to dig down deep into myself and felt that my last year of dealing with the Bush Fellowship for leadership had set me up for just this moment in time.

So, I called Johnny back and told him if he could give me some control over his studios, I would do the show myself, which meant lights, costumes, staging, music, tickets, backdrops, transportation, and recruiting adults for the opening act. Johnny was shocked that I would take on the whole project by myself, but I felt good about my decision. I reviewed and signed every check for anything that dealt with the Nutcracker in the next four months.

I wore several hats for this project. There were times when I would get home around 7:30 and would have a call from Aberdeen or Huron because they had a problem. It needed my attention, so I would jump in my car and drive 100 miles to fix the problem. While the work on the Nutcracker was done every day, I still had other responsibilities, such as teaching, conducting the Youth Symphony, and playing viola in the Northern College Symphony and SDSU Symphony Orchestra in Brookings under John Colson. Then there arose a situation with my son.

My oldest son Michael was a 9th grader; in middle school, he was concertmaster of the orchestra, not because he was my son, but because he earned that spot. I was Michael's only teacher until the past summer, and I started him on violin when he was four years old. The high school teacher did not want 9th graders to try out for the All-State Orchestra because she did not think they would be ready to audition. Still, when I had the 9th graders, it was something that we took pride in to be able to make All-State. When I had the 9th grade, Watertown would have 15-20 students make All-State, but after we went to a middle school, the numbers dropped to 7-10. So, the previous summer I sent Michael to another string teacher in the area to work with him, but I still worked with him on All-State material.

When the school year started, Michael was sitting in the last chair in the violin section, and the high school teacher did not want him to try out for All-State. As a parent and teacher, I put my foot down on this and asked her to let Michael audition; she said she would, but that he was not All-State material. Michael auditioned and was selected as principal second violin leader, and every other Watertown violin player sat behind Michael. I was proud of him for the work he put in and how he handled the high school situation.

The All-State trip did have a lot of drama. We were headed out to Rapid City, three hundred miles away. I was riding on the All-state Orchestra and Choir bus because I was past president of ASTA and had duties with the other string teachers across the state. At that point, the two high school teachers told me in front of all students that only players could ride the bus. I had to call my principal to get them to let me on the bus, which they did.

When we got to Rapid City, I went to get my room key, and they told me that the high school choir teacher and I would be sharing a room together, but he never showed up in the room. He chose another room because he did not want to share a room with me. This was hurtful, and I reported it to the administrators. When we got back, they called the three of us in for a meeting, but nothing was ever done about the situation.

After leading his section in All-State, my son was still sitting in the last chair in the high school orchestra. Any student at the high school studying with Mr. Scales was also sitting in the back of the orchestra. I talked to my principal about this situation, and I told him that it had to change because my second son would be playing the cello at the high school next year. Jason was not as mild as Michael, and she would genuinely have a problem with him, so I wrote an eight-page letter to the high school director. In the letter, I expressed my feelings about the past few years and wanted to see if we could work things out because it was now affecting the program and the students.

I finished the letter, took it over to the high school, and put it in her box. By the end of the day, I had the letter back in my mailbox, so I went to my office and sat down to read her response. I opened the letter to find eight pages of circled red marks all throughout my letter. She had graded my heart-felt letter like I was a little kid. I was hurt and humiliated by her actions. I also felt discriminated against because she would not have done this to a white person.

I took the letter to my principal and told him that I wanted to file a formal complaint against this teacher for racial discrimination and the racial harassment of my son. The principal said he would set up a meeting with the high school principal. I had a ninety-minute meeting in my office with the high school principal the next day. The principal asked questions and took notes. I knew the principal quite well because he was one of the adult dancers in the Nutcracker, which was now two weeks away. He said that he would have a meeting with the Superintendent and that they would get back to me.

Three days before Thanksgiving, I had to call a company in Pittsburgh that made snow machine boxes for our winter scene because they were a week late. The owner said he was sorry, but they had rented them all out, and mine was not listed. He told me they were easy to make and gave me the measurements to design the boxes. I ran over to Mel's garage (my father-in-law), where he and his friends had coffee every morning, laid the box design in front of them, and asked how long it would take to design it. Mel said, "Come back at noon."

I came back at noon, and they had it built. I made them the official snow group, and they ran the snow machine for all the shows. I called them the snow technicians.

The day after Thanksgiving, we had our first full rehearsal, and it went well. Everyone left with a great sense of pride, and after the second rehearsal, I knew that it would be an outstanding program. The first show was on December 3rd in Aberdeen. The three backdrops for the show were scheduled to be loaded on a plane from L.A. on December 2nd, arriving in Watertown at 10:00 a.m. on December 3rd.

I had a funny feeling about the backdrops arriving on time, so I called the shipping company, and they said that the backdrops were there. However, the person responsible for getting them to the airport was not coming in that day. I spent an hour on the phone persuading this person to deliver the backdrops to the airport because our first show was the next day. I explained the whole process I had gone through to put this performance on and how many people were involved. After hearing the story, the clerk said that he would take them to the airport himself, and the following day I could pick the backdrops up at the Watertown airport.

The Nutcracker Weekend

The first day of the *Nutcracker* was here; it was the morning of December 3, 1999, and I had taken a personal leave day from school. I had to pick up the U-Haul truck at 8:00 a.m. because I was the equipment man, and I had to load and drive the truck to each event. Two guys were there to help me pack, and the truck was loaded to the top. After loading, I then drove out to the airport to pick up the three backdrops that were to be on the 10:00 flight from Minneapolis and thank God they were there. I then drove to the middle school and the high school to pick up Michael & Jason. They were going with me to Aberdeen to help unload and set the stage up for the evening performance. They both had their instruments; Michael played 2nd violin, and Jason played cello. It would be a long day for my boys. We got to Aberdeen by noon and stopped to have a bite to eat. We were setting up by 12:15, and it was a slow process. I looked at my watch, and it was 2:00, which meant that it had begun.

At 2:00, I had two chartered buses leaving Watertown (a 100-mile trip) with the student and adult dancers. In Huron, I had one chartered bus (100-mile trip) leaving with kids and adults headed to Aberdeen. The buses were at the performance hall by 4:00, and I had meals set up for everyone before we started to get dressed for the dress rehearsal. We did a light rehearsal to familiarize ourselves with the stage and the three backdrops.

The time was now 7:15, and I was making my last contact with my leaders backstage and with the chaperones back in the rooms where the students were when they were not on stage. My whole family was involved in this production. Martha, Michael, and Jason were in the pit orchestra, Caitlin was one of the Gingerbread Girls, and Matthew was Fritz.

I made it back to the pit, and it was five minutes before showtime. I looked around at the orchestra and saw that they were not comfortable sitting in a strange pit and performing in a place they didn't know. Remember, the orchestra players' ages ranged from 14-to 84. Most of the high school players were my students, but this was the original *Nutcracker* score. We would be playing for over two hours, and the thing I worried about the most was mental fatigue. The baton dropped at 7:30, and the show began. Everything went smoothly until we finished the party and mouse scene when the Nutcracker became a real person. Clara and the Nutcracker were standing in front of a closed curtain, waiting for the winter scene to change. The curtain did not open on cue, so I had to give the circle back sign to the orchestra so we would not run out of music, and it worked out great. No problems after that, but if I had to give this concert a grade, it would have been a B-.

The audience really enjoyed our production, and I felt good about it, but I knew we could do better. The show was done, and I had buses going back to Watertown and Huron. Two hours later, I had the truck loaded up, and my two boys and I were headed to Huron because my family had rooms in Huron for the night. The next day we would be in our own hall with our own audience. I was immensely proud of my family, and we were all exhausted.

December 4, 1999

The day called for a 3:00 dress rehearsal, so Watertown had two buses leaving at 1:00. Aberdeen had one bus loading and going at 1:00. I started the stage set up at 11:00, and it was much easier this time and did not take as long. At 3:00 I had everyone out on stage. I explained that we would not be rehearsing the whole show because of the show's duration but would be touching on parts that might need attention. Plus, I knew that fatigue could be a factor with some players.

The assistant choreographer, Bridget from Charlotte, North Carolina, disagreed with me and wanted to run through the entire show. I again explained my reasoning for the spot-check rehearsal. But she did disagree and said out loud to my leaders and everyone else on the stage, "Who can fix this for me?"

I told everyone to take a five-minute break and told Bridget we needed to talk. I did not have the time to get into a debate with her, so

I asked her whose name was on her contract and whose name was on her checks. She acknowledged that my name was on both, so I gave her two options.

The first was that we go back out on stage, and she could pick any sections that she thought needed attention, and the second option was that I could have someone run her back to the hotel and then drive her to the airport. I went back on stage, and a minute later, Bridget came on stage, and we had a great rehearsal.

It was now 7:20, and the auditorium had over 1100 people in their seats. The orchestra was tuning, and I noticed two of my horn players (two high school players) were not tuning. They were engaged in conversation with people from the audience. I walked back to the two players and told them that I did not think they were getting mentally prepared for the show and reminded them of how vital their parts were. I turned and walked away because there was nothing else to say, and I knew they understood.

The baton dropped at 7:30, and from the start of the show, we had more energy than the previous night. The night felt like a home game. The dancers smiled more as they danced, and the orchestra played with confidence. Everything was spot on during the show, and the curtain for the winter scene was right on time.

The Land of the Sweets scene brought the audience to life. (You can see the whole third movement of the *Nutcracker* on my YouTube channel—Conductor Phil Scales). The two professional dancers were outstanding. Tonight's show was top-notch, and the audience showed their gratitude by staying until the last note was played (you can see this at the end of the video). When the show ended, I went back to my horn section and told the girls that they did a fantastic job and I was proud of them, and I shook their hands. The breakdown was much faster this time, and my family stayed overnight in Huron and hit our beds at midnight. The next day in Watertown, we would have a matinee and an evening show.

December 5, 1999

The following day was an early rise for my family. We had breakfast and were on the road by 8:00. We had 100 miles to drive, and the setup started at 11:00. The buses also began to roll at 11:00. I had a charter bus leaving Aberdeen and a bus leaving Huron. The buses should be in Watertown by 1:00, and we had a light snack for everyone. I felt that we did not need any kind of rehearsal because everyone had been on this stage before. After all, this was where we had our dress rehearsal in the beginning.

I was excited about performing in Watertown because this was home. This is where the dream of doing the *Nutcracker* started. The two shows in Watertown were sold out (1200 people a show), and I thought of Ms. Marghab and wished that she could hear the Watertown Symphony perform today.

It was 1:45, and I was called to the back of the auditorium to find the Fire Marshal. He said that there were more people than seats, so we put several rows of seats in the back and left the back door open for safety. I ran down the hall at 1:55 to get to the pit. It was now showtime.

The whole cast and orchestra kept the energy from the night before, and the shows were magical. The audience gave both shows a standing ovation, and it was well deserved. I wished my mom or family members could have seen my work because I was the "Black orchestra teacher" when I started in Watertown, but now they called me "Mr. Scales." This show was the highlight of my career, and I walked into my home well after midnight.

I lay in bed that night and told Martha that I did not think I could do any more here and felt it was time to move our kids to a place where they would have more diversity in their lives. I was tired of fighting for everything I wanted and tired of seeing students being mistreated because of me. I still had not heard back from the high school principal about my meeting with him. The two older boys had been running into a few racial problems lately, and it was time to put them at the top of my list. Martha agreed, and I was at total peace for the first time in a while. I thought of Johnny and how proud he must be of his dancers, because I sure was.

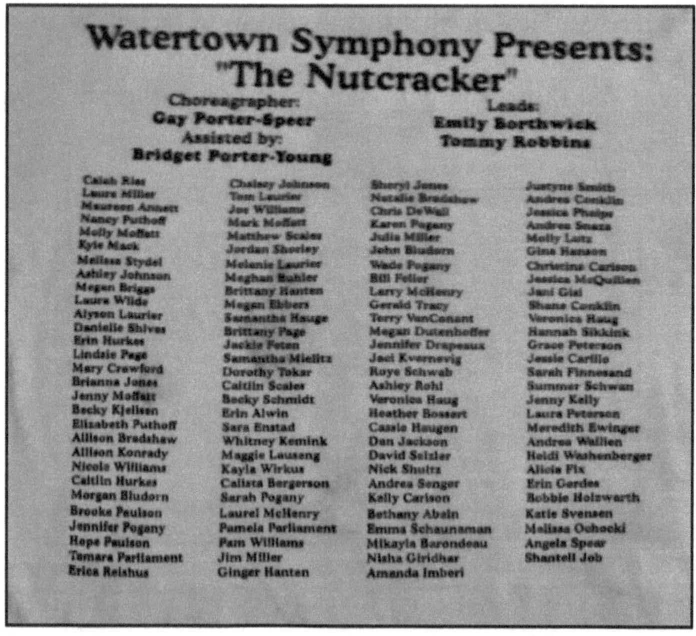

Watertown Symphony Presents:
"The Nutcracker"

Choreographer:
Gay Porter-Speer
Assisted by:
Bridget Porter-Young

Leads:
Emily Borthwick
Tommy Robbins

Caleb Ries	Chalsey Johnson	Sheryl Jones	Justyne Smith
Laura Miller	Tom Laurier	Natalie Bradshaw	Andrea Conklin
Maureen Annett	Joe Williams	Chris DeWall	Jessica Phelps
Nancy Puthoff	Mark Moffatt	Karen Pogany	Andrea Snaza
Molly Moffett	Matthew Scales	Julia Miller	Molly Lutz
Kyle Mack	Jordan Shorey	John Bludorn	Gina Hanson
Melissa Stydel	Melanie Laurier	Wade Pogany	Christina Carlson
Ashley Johnson	Meghan Buhler	Bill Feller	Jessica McQuillen
Megan Briggs	Brittany Hanten	Larry McHenry	Jani Gisi
Laura Wilde	Megan Ebbers	Gerald Tracy	Shana Conklin
Alyson Laurier	Samantha Hauge	Terry VanConant	Veronica Haug
Danielle Shives	Brittany Page	Megan Dutenhoffer	Hannah Sikkink
Erin Hurkes	Jackie Foten	Jennifer Drapeaux	Grace Peterson
Lindsie Page	Samantha Mielitz	Jaci Kvernevig	Jessie Carlile
Mary Crawford	Dorothy Tokar	Roye Schwab	Sarah Finnesand
Brianna Jones	Caitlin Scales	Ashley Rohl	Summer Schwan
Jenny Moffatt	Becky Schmidt	Veronica Haug	Jenny Kelly
Becky Kjellsen	Erin Alwin	Heather Bossart	Laura Peterson
Elizabeth Puthoff	Sara Enstad	Cassie Haugen	Meredith Ewinger
Allison Bradshaw	Whitney Kemink	Dan Jackson	Andrea Wullien
Allison Konrady	Maggie Lauseng	David Seizler	Heidi Washenberger
Nicole Williams	Kayla Wirkus	Nick Shultz	Alicia Fix
Caitlin Hurkes	Calista Bergerson	Andrea Senger	Erin Gerdes
Morgan Bludorn	Sarah Pogany	Kelly Carlson	Bobbie Holzwarth
Brooke Paulson	Laurel McHenry	Bethany Abain	Katie Svensen
Jennifer Pogany	Pamela Parliament	Emma Schaunaman	Melissa Ochocki
Hope Paulson	Pam Williams	Mikayla Barondeau	Angela Spear
Tamara Parliament	Jim Miller	Nisha Giridhar	Shantell Job
Erica Reishus	Ginger Hanten	Amanda Imberi	

Closure of the Nutcracker

The project was not over yet for me because I had a lot of work still facing me. I had to finalize all the bills, paying the bus lines, paying for the meals for the kids, returning rental music, storing the costumes and props, returning the rental truck and the backdrops, along with making sure that everyone was paid. After paying all the bills, the Huron Symphony and the Watertown Symphony made a nice profit. I had not had time to reflect yet on the past four months of this project, because I still had a middle-school orchestra concert and the orchestra's annual grade-school Christmas tour of seven grade schools.

The Nutcracker was a great hit in Watertown. I got a lot of personal calls from people in the community and my orchestra members. My principal, who did go to the show, said he thought it was excellent. I met Johnny at Perkins restaurant, and we embraced. He thanked me for all the work that I did, and I thanked him for his outstanding work with his dancers. I thought of the Bush Fellowship and how hard I worked to win as I left the restaurant. But even though I ended up falling short, that experience had given me the confidence that I needed to run the Nutcracker project. But deep in my heart, I knew it was time to move on.

The next day as I was leaving for school, I looked at Martha and told her to find a place for us to move. She looked at me and said, "where?" and I said, "Baby, I'll follow you anywhere" (actual words). I came home for lunch, and Martha picked out Madison, Wisconsin. We had good friends in La Crosse, WI (Mark & Sandy), and Sandy had suggested Madison because we were a professional and artistic family and would fit right into that city. Madison had been named the number one city in the United States in 1999, and we made plans to visit the city over the Christmas holiday to see if it would be a good fit for our family. When my middle-school orchestra took the stage for their Christmas concert, they played in front of 3,000 people between October and the Christmas concert. Our program was over an hour long, ending with a standing ovation. In three days, I would be able to relax with my family and genuinely enjoy the Christmas holidays.

Chapter Ten
The Unthinkable Happens

The day before Christmas break, the principal stopped me in the hall and said that the Superintendent would like me to drop by and see him during the Christmas break. I told the principal that I really did not want to take time from my family and asked if he could do it before the break. A while later, my principal said that the meeting would be tomorrow after school, and I thanked him for getting it changed. I was glad that I would finally have this important discussion about the negative letter I had received, but I decided not to mention the meeting to Martha until it was over.

The next day was an exceptionally long day for me. Every confrontation that I had had with the high school director over the last 14 years ran through my mind. Still, I had great hopes that we would start to change things around after this. I went to the meeting, and my middle school principal was there, along with the high school principal and the Superintendent.

The Superintendent started the meeting with me by saying, "We have a complaint that you asked a student for a kiss two years ago."

At first, I did not think I heard him correctly, and I said, "Excuse me?"

But he did not answer, so I looked at my middle school principal, a man who had always been in my corner, and he could not look at me. I did not know what to say, but I said, "This is not why I am here."

I asked about the meeting I had with the high school principal and what they were going to do about that issue?

The Superintendent replied that this was the only issue on the table. I did not try to defend myself because I knew that this had never happened, but I could see where this was going. I asked the Superintendent what was next, and he said that at the next school board meeting (1-16-2000), he might bring this up, but if I resigned, he would not. I asked about my conducting the Symphony and Youth Symphony in the junior high room if I was no longer teaching. He said that I could still hold my rehearsals in the room on Tuesday evenings and Saturday mornings.

I was in utter shock, and that was how the meeting ended. I went out to my car and cried for a long time. It was three days before Christmas, and there was no way I could tell Martha about this until Christmas was over, so I kept this horrible news to myself for five days. When I finally told Martha about the meeting, we both broke down crying, but then we started looking at our options. The first option was to fight the ridiculous charge, but it would also go to the newspaper if it went to the board. And this would affect our children, and we did not want that.

Our second option was for me to resign. Still, I did not trust the Superintendent to keep his word. So, I went to a lawyer in town (who had helped me set up the bylaws for the Watertown Symphony) and explained everything to him. He advised me to go to the union lawyer because the high school orchestra teacher's husband was Vice President of one of the banks in Watertown. He thought it would be best to go to an out-of-town lawyer.

I went to my union lawyer, and we set up an agreement with the Superintendent in writing that he would not bring this allegation to the board if I resigned. The day before I handed in my resignation, Martha and I took our oldest boys out to dinner (Michael was in 9th grade, and Jason was in 8th grade). I explained what was going on and that I was turning in my resignation and that we would be moving to Madison after they finished the school year. To my surprise, they were pleased to hear that we would be moving. If I could go back and change one thing about that night, I would have told Jason that we would be pulling him out of the middle school for homeschooling because the teachers did not protect my son. He had a hard time in middle school for the rest of the year.

I turned in my resignation the next day, went to the school, and cleaned out all my personal items. It felt funny that I did not teach there anymore. Still, I had both my Watertown Symphony and Youth Symphony rehearsals in the same middle school room. That night I got a call from the board president of the Huron Symphony, and she said that she had a complaint that I verbally harassed two high school students at the *Nutcracker* concert (the two horn players). I needed to give them a public apology, and then they would decide if they would renew my contract at the end of the season.

I did not see a need to apologize to the students, as I had told them what they needed to do that night to succeed for themselves and the orchestra. I told her that I could help her with that decision immediately, as she would have my resignation in the mail by the end of the week.

As I hung up, I felt horrible that I would never get to say goodbye to many beautiful people in the orchestra, who gave me their absolute best every time I stepped on that podium. I took the Huron Symphony farther than they would ever go. The Symphony went dark a year later, opened again for a while but is now dark forever. I always thought it was suspicious that I would get this call the same day I resigned from Watertown.

Martha and I drove to Madison, Wisconsin, to explore our future new home a week later. We fell in love with it, mainly with the diversity. We later took the two older boys to Madison and visited all the high schools to see which school the boys liked the best. They picked James Madison Memorial High School on the west side of Madison, and I paid a six-month lease on a five-bedroom apartment that day. The plan was to move things over to Madison during the remaining school year.

I was still directing the Watertown Symphony on Tuesday nights and the Youth Symphony on Saturday mornings. The Youth Symphony had already planned a trip, and the kids had been fundraising since September. I told my Youth Symphony players why I resigned, and I told them about the allegation and said, "For those of you who study privately with me, you can agree that our lessons never got that good."

And that broke the ice for the rehearsal. I lost only one student, and her dad was a close friend of the Superintendent.

People's Court

I tried to keep busy every day by taking the kids to school and packing things up for our move. I would go to the gym at noon because there was always an adult pickup basketball game going on, and this would allow me to let off some steam. I then got interested in watching Judge Mathis and People's Court every day until it was time to pick up the kids. One day I got a call from the one student whose father had pulled her out of the group, and he wanted her money back from the fundraisers she had participated in. I told her to tell her father that the money stayed with the group and was split evenly between the group members.

He did not like my answer, and two weeks later, I got a letter from the court saying that I was being sued for keeping the student's fundraising money and it had a court date on it. I went to court with Martha and Trevor M. by my side. Trevor was now a sophomore in college, and I started him in 5th grade. He was part of the Youth Symphony for many years and went on many of our trips, so he would speak on behalf of the group. I had all the paperwork that I needed, and I was ready to defend the Youth Symphony.

The judge called the young lady to the stand and asked what she said to people when she was fundraising. The student said she told them what she was selling and asked if they wanted to buy it. The judge asked her if she said who she was selling the products for, and the student said she was selling them for the Youth Symphony trip. I knew where this was going, and the judge said that her son was in the Brookings band. They sold fruit for their trip, and he represented the Brookings band, but if he did not go on the trip, the money would stay with the band. Therefore, this case was dismissed. The three of us walked to the parking lot, and as we got to the car, we let out a huge cheer, only to turn around and discover that the father was parked right next to us.

A day at the gym

I really enjoyed going to the gym because it kept my mind positive and helped the time go by. It was February now, and there were many people at the gym, and one of them was my pastor. I had not seen him in 5 weeks. I stopped going to church because the Superintendent attended the same church that we went to. I ran four games with my pastor, and as I was leaving, he came over and asked how I was doing. I said that my family was not doing well and that my minister had let us down because he should have been at my house a long time ago with prayers, whether he thought I was guilty or not. "You are my pastor," I told him, "and you let my family and me down."

I was the only Black man in that church, and I taught Sunday school and supported the church with my heart and money. I turned and walked away; forty minutes later, there was a knock on my door, and it was the pastor. He said that I was right. He should have been here earlier, and he stayed for about an hour.

157

March Symphony Concert

I had already been back to Madison several times, taking things to our new home, but the next concert was upon us. One of my good friends at Northern University, Dr. Matthew James, the vocal teacher and an outstanding baritone, was featured in the March concert. I didn't know what kind of response I would get as far as attendance for the show because I was no longer teaching. We usually got between 400 and 600 people at the concerts (except when we did the *Nutcracker* or the *Messiah*, when we drew over a thousand people). Still, we pulled over 700 people for this concert, which was exciting. Dr. James sang the *Marriage of Figaro*, *La Vendetta*, and *Non-Piu Andrai*.

He also did *Ella Giammai M'Amo* by Verdi and *La Calunnia* (The Barber of Seville) by Rossini, which brought the audience to their feet. The orchestra ended the concert's first half with *Overture to Fidelio* by Beethoven, and then we ended the concert with *Overture to Nabucco* by Verdi, which had the audience on their feet for a second standing ovation. I had wanted to end on a positive note, but I did not expect this response. I did what I always did after a concert, and personally thanked every player on stage for their hard work and support for the Watertown Symphony and me. This concert was extraordinary because everyone knew what my family was going through, and they were there to support us. It was a good day.

Protecting My Children

I had been in Watertown for 14 years, and it was a good community, but every now and then, racism would raise its ugly head. I had been up to the middle school on two occasions since January because students had called my son the N-word, and nothing was done. I shocked the middle-school teachers when Martha and I showed up at parent-teacher meetings. The school district was just getting fully involved on the internet, and the students thought it was great that they could email each other in school. But someone began sending my son threatening and intimidating emails through the school system in high school because he was Black.

I called the high school principal and asked to find out who was doing this, but he refused to investigate. So, I called the Sioux Falls chapter of the NAACP and left messages for three days and never got a response. I finally reached the principal again and told him that if he didn't try and find out who was sending these messages, I would call the FBI. I got a call from the principal two hours later, and he said that they had found the person and that he was suspended. They gave me the student's name, but I was upset that I was made to jump through so many hoops to protect my son.

A New Rehearsal Place

A few days after the email situation, I got a letter from the Superintendent that said that I could no longer rehearse the Youth Symphony at the middle school on Saturday mornings, although it said nothing about rehearsing the Watertown Symphony in the same room on Tuesday nights. The Youth Symphony was scheduled to tour the Eastern Seaboard in 9 weeks, and we still had 8 rehearsals. I went to the Best Western Hotel to see if they would let me rent the conference room next to the pool on Saturdays for two hours, and they agreed. So, the Youth Symphony members would meet at the hotel for the next 8 rehearsals (at $60.00 per rehearsal, which I paid). I would get there early and set up all the wire stands and chairs. I did not get paid for the Youth Symphony, but these were my students, and I would do anything for them.

Last Symphony Concert

Three weeks before my last concert with the Watertown Symphony, it started to weigh on me. I didn't know how I would feel knowing that this group may never play again after this concert. With Huron, the players and I left on a high note with the *Nutcracker* performance. But with Watertown, it could get emotional. I had many former students coming in to play at my last concert, so I would enjoy that, but the overall concert, well, I just didn't know.

I had everything lined up for the final push. After the concert, there would be a reception for Martha and me, put on by the Symphony Board. The next day Martha and I would board a plane to London, England, for a needed respite for both of us. Once back, I would have four weeks before our final Youth Symphony concert. I had no idea where we would play because I was locked out of any performing areas where we could play, but that was a problem I would worry about later.

The last thing on the list was the Youth Symphony's upcoming trip, and then my family would leave Watertown two days later.

The concert was here, and I was standing backstage, ready to take the podium, and no one was around but the stage manager, and I lost it. My body started to shake, my eyes teared up, and I had shortness of breath to the point I had to walk outside for a moment. I got it together, went back inside, and walked out to the podium. I picked up my baton and realized that I had my gold coin in my hand, and I couldn't remember when I got it out of my pocket. I looked around at all the faces in the orchestra, and I made eye contact with Dr. Bob (concertmaster) and then Martha, who sat next to him on the first stand.

I was now ready for my last concert, and the baton went up. The crowd was over 500 hundred people, and they really enjoyed the show. We were playing the final number, and mid-performance, I thought that this might be the last concert that the Watertown symphony would ever perform, which, of course, made me very sad. When the concert finished, and I gave my final cut-off, the audience began to clap. I then walked straight into the viola section and handed my baton to my former student Trevor.

I never told him why I gave him my baton, but I felt that if this was the last cut-off for the Watertown Symphony, I wanted him to have that baton. I then walked over, shook hands with Dr. Bob, kissed my lovely wife, took my bow, and left the stage. The audience gave me three curtain calls, which all were very emotional, and then I did what I would do after every concert. I stood at the stage door and personally thanked and shook every player's hand. The reception was outstanding, but it did get emotional, and when we left, I was totally drained.

The next day we got up, and we were off to London. The trip was just what we needed - time alone together. Since this was our second trip to London, we knew exactly where we wanted to go. Because on the first trip I was responsible for 80 people we really couldn't do many things we would have liked to do. We found a nice quiet Italian restaurant, and we would spend two and a half hours at dinner, downing a nice bottle of wine and enjoying each other's company. We went to this restaurant three nights in a row, and on the third night when we walked in the owner sent over a bottle of wine on him. He said that he loved to see a couple that really enjoyed each other's company. This trip was just what we needed to mentally prepare for our final push towards our move, and now we were on the plane headed back to the States.

Finding a Place to Play

We had three more rehearsals at the motel before our last Youth Symphony concert, but we didn't have a place to perform the concert. So, I went to the Watertown Mall and arranged for the group to play in front of the Herberger's department store. The last three rehearsals went very well. Everyone was ready and excited to perform our final concert of the year. On the day of the concert, we were warming up to adjust to the acoustics in the open space. I had chairs set up for parents and followers of the Youth Symphony. As we finished warming up, I stepped to the back of the group so the concertmistress could get the orchestra tuned up and ready to go.

My former principal walked up to me and said, "The kids sound great."

I was stunned because this was the last person I expected to see, and he acted as if nothing had happened. I paused for a second, caught myself, and replied, "Thank you," then I walked to the podium, and started the program.

The concert ended on a very high note. I looked around at all the people who showed up or stopped to listen to the group. I noticed that not one teacher had shown up to hear these outstanding students play for the last time, but of course this was the standard over the previous nine years.

The Eastern Seaboard

This would be our eighth straight Youth Symphony trip, and it would be the last. My objective for these South Dakota kids was to allow them to get out of South Dakota, see some of the world and have a life-learning experience through music. I wanted them to have the chance to meet kids from different parts of the state and develop long-term friendships with them; this part undoubtedly happened. We would fly to Boston on our last trip and get on a charter bus. We would spend two days in Boston, three days in New York, one day in Philly, two days in D.C., two days in Williamsburg, and a day at Busch Gardens amusement park. We would then fly back to South Dakota. This would be a significant trip for Tish because he had an engagement ring burning a hole in his pocket, and he was trying to pick the right place to propose to Cindy. They had been dating for a few years, and Cindy was a chaperone for several of our trips, so Tish would propose to her somewhere down the road. The students got a kick out of Boston, going to the "Cheers Bar" and Faneuil Hall Marketplace. New York was fantastic to the students, and one day we stepped out in our finest clothes to attend a performance of *Footloose* on Broadway.

We were standing in line to get into *Footloose*, and a group of us got together for a picture. These two older ladies asked some of the chaperones where the group was from, and they said South Dakota. One of the ladies then said, "Isn't that so nice of Al (Al Roker) to take that picture with this group from South Dakota?"

Youth Symphony and Al Roker (not!)

The day in Philly was a lot of fun. We stopped the bus at the famous Rocky steps, and I jumped off the bus and ran up the steps. When I reached the top, I fell on my back, and the kids got a big kick out of that, but seriously it really hurt - I was really hurting. The next day we were off to Washington, D.C. It was indeed an excellent experience for these South Dakota students. As we walked around the monuments, we stopped at the Lincoln Memorial, and Tish dropped to one knee and proposed to Cindy. All the girls thought it was the most romantic thing they had ever witnessed.

Guess who the best man was?

I was so happy for my friend, and I was glad that he was with me on every trip. We were a great team, and I was proud and honored to be his best man. The next day was nothing but fun because Busch Gardens is one of the best amusement parks in the United States, and we had a blast. The next day we were off to the airport for our flight back to South Dakota.

We arrived back at the middle school on a Friday night, and a few miles from the middle school, it began to hit the students that this was it and we would be parting soon. I could hear the tears start, and as the kids got off the bus, I gave each of them a hug and thanked them for their years of support. I kept everything in check until the parents came up to me, and I knew that it was over, and no one would ever start the program again. Then it began to hurt inside, and I gave Tish a hug, and it was over.

Packing up

I got up the following day with two days to pack the U-Haul and move to Madison, but that morning I woke up with the worst gout attack I had had in a few years. My left big toe was throbbing, and my left ankle joint was so swollen that I didn't think I could walk, but the move had to go on. My helpers were my sons, Michael, and Jason.

We did get help from my brother-in-law Bruce and Travis B., and Katie E. These two students were Michael and Jason's friends from grade school and were also part of my string family (violin players). The first loading day was very hard, primarily because of my gout attack. Still, the lack of help was also disappointing. I had lived in this town for 14 years, and yet not one teacher offered to help my family. When I began teaching in Watertown, Martha and I would invite teachers over for dinner or drinks to get to know them better. I was never invited to any teachers' homes, not even my principal, who I looked up to. The next day I walked out of my front door at 6:15 to finish the loading. Travis and Katie were sitting on my step. We were exhausted by 8:30 a.m. and on the road by 9:00 a.m. We had everything done except sweeping the floor, and Martha's mom said she would finish that part for us because we had an eight-hour drive ahead of us. As we were getting ready to leave, I thanked Travis and Katie for all their help and for being such great kids.

It was hard to say goodbye to Mom and Mel (Martha's parents) because they were great people and the kids loved them dearly. I couldn't turn my mind off as we headed down the interstate. Martha was driving the car with Caitlin, Matthew, and Belle, our Shih-Tzu. I had Michael and Jason in the truck with me. After several hours of traveling, we hit the Wisconsin border, and I laughed out loud because we didn't have any jobs lined up. Still, it didn't matter because we had faith, family, and skills.

I also started to think of the people that helped me keep moving during some of the hard times in Watertown. These men were great thinkers - Norman Vincent Peale, Napoleon Hill, and W. Clement Stone. Mr. Stone was a great believer in PMA., a Positive Mental Attitude. I also believed in this great quote from him: *"Wealth is created through the positive mental attitude, education, labor, knowledge, know-how, and moral character of people."*

Napoleon Hill has a quote that has guided me through my life every day: *"What Your Mind Can Conceive and Believe, It Can Achieve."*

I tapped that coin in my pocket and said,
I Believe I Can Fly.

To be continued.